# Contents

*Business Vocabulary in Use (advanced)*    **5**

## Cambridge International Corpus

In writing this book, extensive use has been made of business-related material from the Cambridge International Corpus: business articles from the British and American press. The corpus has provided valuable information on the typical patterns of business English usage, and this has been used in compiling the language presentation material and in many of the exercises.

The Cambridge International Corpus is a vast database of over 700 million words of real English taken from books, newspapers, advertising, letters and emails, websites, conversations and speeches, radio and television.

- The Corpus helps us to get a representative picture of how English is used, both in writing and in speech

- It is constantly being updated so we are able to include new words in our books as soon as they appear.

- It contains both British and American English, which means we can analyse the differences and produce accurate materials based on either variety of English.

- It is 'real' English so we can ensure that examples in our books are natural and realistic.

## Cambridge Business Corpus

The Cambridge Business Corpus, which is part of the Cambridge International Corpus, contains business articles from the British and American press, business books, financial and legal documents, company reports, professional and commercial texts, government reports and product descriptions.

More choice from the world's bestsellers http://www.cambridge.org/elt/inuse

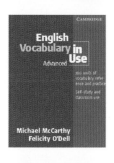

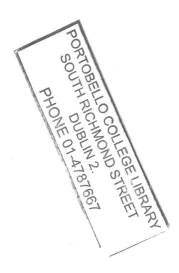

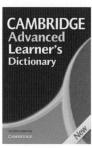

Visit our dictionary website:
www.dictionary.cambridge.org

# Introduction

## Who is this book for?

*Business Vocabulary in Use Advanced* builds on the success of *Business Vocabulary in Use*. It is designed to help upper-intermediate and advanced learners of business English improve their business vocabulary. It is for people studying English before they start work and for those already working who need English in their job.

The emphasis is on language related to today's important, and sometimes controversial, business issues.

You can use the book on your own for self-study, or with a teacher in the classroom, one-to-one or in groups.

## How is the book organized?

The book contains 50 two-page thematic units, in eight key business areas.

The left-hand page of each unit presents and explains new words and expressions, and the right-hand page allows you to check and develop your understanding of them and how they are used through a series of exercises.

There is **cross-referencing** between units to show connections between uses of the same word or similar words used in different contexts.

There is an **answer key** at the back of the book. Most of the exercises have questions with only one correct answer. But some of the exercises, including the **Over to you** activities at the end of each unit (see below), are designed for discussion and/or writing about yourself and your own organization or one you would like to work for.

Where appropriate, **references** at the bottom of left-hand pages give the sources (books and websites) for the ideas under discussion.

There is also an **index**. This lists all the new words and phrases introduced in the book and gives the unit numbers where they appear. The index also tells you how the words and expressions are pronounced.

## The left-hand page

This page introduces the new vocabulary and expressions for each thematic area. The presentation is divided into a number of sections indicated by letters: A, B, C, with simple, clear titles.

As well as explanations of vocabulary, there is information about:

- typical word combinations.
- the grammar associated with particular vocabulary, for example the verbs that are used with particular nouns.

There are also notes on tricky language points, such as countable and uncountable nouns, and the differences between British and American English.

# Business
# Vocabulary in Use
# Advanced

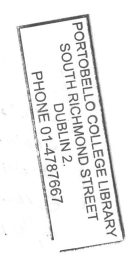

## CAMBRIDGE
### UNIVERSITY PRESS

CAMBRIDGE UNIVERSITY PRESS
Cambridge, New York, Melbourne, Madrid, Cape Town, Singapore, São Paulo, Delhi

Cambridge University Press
The Edinburgh Building, Cambridge CB2 8RU, UK

www.cambridge.org
Information on this title: www.cambridge.org/9780521540704

First published 2004
6th printing 2008

Printed in Dubai by Oriental Press

*A catalogue record for this publication is available from the British Library*

ISBN 978-0-521-54070-4 paperback

## The right-hand page

The exercises on the right-hand page give practice in using the new vocabulary and expressions presented on the left-hand page. Sometimes the exercises concentrate on using the words and expressions presented on the left-hand page in context. Other exercises practise the grammatical forms of items from the left-hand page. Some units contain tables to complete, or crosswords.

## 'Over to you' activities

An important feature of *Business Vocabulary in Use Advanced* is the **Over to you** activity at the end of each unit, which caters for learners who are in work as well as those who are not. The **Over to you** activities give you the chance to put into practice the words and expressions in the unit in relation to your own professional situation, studies or opinions.

Self-study learners can do this as a written activity.

In the classroom, the **Over to you** activities can be used as the basis for discussion with the whole class, or in small groups with a spokesperson for each group summarizing the discussion and its outcome for the class. The teacher can then get learners to look again at the words and expressions that have caused difficulty. Learners can follow up by using the **Over to you** as a written activity, for example as homework.

## How to use the book for self-study

Find the topic you are looking for by referring to the contents page or the index. Read through the explanations on the left-hand page of the unit. Do the exercises on the right-hand page. Check your answers in the key. If you have made some mistakes, go back and look at the explanations and exercise again. Note down important words and expressions in your notebook.

## How to use the book in the classroom

Teachers can choose units that relate to learners' particular needs and interests, for example areas they have covered in course books, or that have come up in other activities. Alternatively, lessons can contain a regular vocabulary slot, where learners look systematically at the vocabulary of particular thematic or skills areas.

Learners can work on the units in pairs, with the teacher going round the class assisting and advising. Teachers should get learners to think about the logical process of the exercises, pointing out why one answer is possible and others are not.

We hope you enjoy using this book.

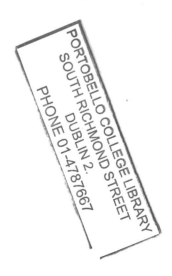

# 1 World of work

## A My work is so rewarding

'I work in advertising. I love my work, which is really **rewarding** and **stimulating**. **Originality** and **creativity** are very important in this industry, of course.

**No two days are the same** in my job: I could be contacting film companies for new advertising campaigns one day and giving client presentations the next. I like the **client contact** and I am very much **hands-on** – being involved with the productive work of the agency rather than managing it.

When I joined the agency, I **hit it off with** my colleagues immediately and I still **get on well with** them. There's a very good **rapport** between us.'

## B I like the team work

'I'm an aircraft engineer. I work on the research and development of new aircraft. I love **putting ideas into practice**. I like **working on my own**, but it's also great being part of a team. I like the **team work** and the **sense of achievement** when we do something new. And of course, the planes we produce are very beautiful.

Is there anything I don't like? I dislike days when I'm **chained to a desk**. I don't like **admin** and **paperwork** – sometimes I feel I'm **snowed under** with it. And in a large organization like ours, there can be a lot of **red tape** and **bureaucracy** – **rigid procedures** that can slow things down.'

## C I want to make a contribution

'I'm a secondary school teacher. It's a low-paid job but I want to help people and **make a contribution to society**. That's what gives me **motivation**. My job gives me a lot of **satisfaction**. The work can be **stretching**, taking me to the limits of my skills and knowledge. But it's great to see kids developing and learning. Of course, they can be very difficult and **demanding**, but sometimes we even get **recognition** from parents that we are doing a good job! But I don't like unnecessary interference – I don't like people **breathing down my neck**.'

**1.1** Complete the sentences with expressions from A opposite.

1 Work that is interesting and exciting is ................ and ................ .

2 If you spend time with customers, you have ................ ................ .

3 If you have a good working relationship with your colleagues, you ................
................ well with them.

4 If you do the actual work of the organization rather than being a manager, you are
................-................ .

5 If you want to say that work is not repetitive, you can say, '................
................ ................ ................ ................'.

6 ................ and ................ are when you have new and effective ideas that
people have not had before.

**1.2** The aircraft engineer talks about his work. Complete his statements with expressions from B opposite.

1
Sometimes I work late at the office when everyone has gone home. I like ................ ................ ................ ................ .

2
It's great to see what I learnt during my engineering course at university being applied in actual designs. I like ................ .

3
I hate it when there is a big stack of documents and letters on my desk that I have to deal with. I don't like ................ and ................ .

4
I love the ................ ................ involved when we all work together to create something new.

5
It's rare, but sometimes when I come into the office and see a huge pile of work waiting for me, I feel completely ................ ................ .

6
When we see a new plane fly for the first time, we all feel a great ................ ................ ................ .

7
I get frustrated when you have to get permission to spend anything over £50. I don't like ................ and ................ ................ .

**1.3** Complete this table with words from C opposite and related forms. Put a stress mark in front of the stressed syllable in each word. (The first one has been done for you.)

| Verb | Noun | Adjective |
| --- | --- | --- |
| con'tribute (or 'contribute) | contri'bution | con'tributory |
| demand | | |
| motivate | | |
| recognize | | |
| satisfy | | |

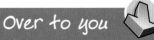

## Over to you

Write a job description for your own job or one you would like, and say why you feel you are suitable for it.

# 2 Management styles 1

## A Motivation 1

Yolanda – senior manager, car rental firm

I believe that all our employees can find **satisfaction** in what they do. We give them **responsibility**, which means that the decisions they take have a direct impact on our success, and encourage them to **use their initiative**, so they don't have to ask me about every decision they make.

We hope this gives employees the feeling that they are **valued**, with management knowing the effort they make. We believe that all this leads to a higher sense of **motivation** among employees.

When everyone feels motivated, **morale** is good and there is a general feeling of **well-being** in the organization.

## B Motivation 2

I don't believe in all this talk about motivation. My **subordinates**, the people **working under me**, are basically lazy and need constant **supervision** – we have to check what they are doing all the time. Some people think this is **authoritarian**, but I think it's the only way of managing.

Decisions must be **imposed** from above without **consultation** – we don't discuss decisions with workers, we just tell them what to do.

Xavier – factory manager

Note: **Subordinate** is very formal and can be negative.

## C Theory X and Theory Y

Xavier has **conservative** views and believes in what the US management thinker Douglas McGregor[1] called **Theory X**, the idea that people dislike work and will do everything they can to avoid it.

Yolanda is more **humanitarian** and believes in **Theory Y**, the more advanced view that, given the right conditions, everyone has the potential to find satisfaction in work.

Others have suggested **Theory W** (for 'whiplash'), the idea that most work since the beginning of human society has been done under systems of slavery.

[1] *The Human Side of Enterprise* (McGraw Hill 1985)

**2.1** Yolanda's employees are talking about her management style – see A opposite. Replace the underlined phrases with appropriate forms of expressions from A. (Pay attention to the grammatical context. The first one has been done for you.)

1 She knows exactly what's involved in our jobs. She makes us feel <u>she understands the effort we make</u>.

*She makes us feel <u>valued</u>.*

2 She encourages us to <u>do things without asking her first</u>.

3 <u>The feeling among employees</u> here is very good. We feel really <u>involved and want</u> to work towards the company's goals.

4 We have a real sense of <u>the idea that our efforts are important for the success of the company</u>.

5 We have a real sense of <u>liking what we do and feeling good when we achieve specific goals</u> in our work.

**2.2** Look at the expressions in B opposite and say if these statements are true or false.

1 Authoritarian managers like listening to the opinions of their employees.

2 If people need constant supervision, you have to watch them all the time.

3 Authoritarian managers like the idea of consultation with their employees.

4 If decisions are imposed from above, employees have no influence over them.

5 Someone's subordinates are the people working above them.

**2.3** Managers from different companies are talking about their employees. Look at C opposite and say whether each manager believes in Theory X or Theory Y.

1
> You have to keep an eye on employees the whole time. I don't allow them to work at home.

2
> It's important to let people work without constant supervision. They feel they're being treated like children otherwise.

3
> I encourage employees to use their own initiative. That way you can see the potential future managers among them.

4
> They must be here by 8.30 am and they can't leave before 5.30 pm. That way I can be sure they are doing the work we are paying them to do.

5
> We encourage the workers at the plant to make suggestions for improvements in the processes they are involved with.

6
> All they're interested in is getting to the weekend, doing as little as possible.

## Over to you

Write a memo to the head of your organization or one you would like to work for, suggesting ways to encourage initiative among employees.

# 3 Management styles 2

## A Hygiene factors

Yolanda, the car rental manager we met in Unit 2, went on a management course. She looked at the work of Frederick Herzberg[1], who studied what motivates employees, and took these notes.

> There are aspects of work that are not in themselves enough to make employees satisfied, but that can cause <u>dissatisfaction</u> if they are not right.
> These are <u>hygiene factors</u>:
> <u>supervision</u> – the way you are managed
> <u>policy</u> – the overall purpose and goals of the organization
> <u>working conditions</u> – the place where you work, hours worked, etc.
> <u>salary</u>
> <u>peer relationships</u> – how you relate to and work with others at the same level in the organization
> <u>security</u> – level of confidence about the future of your job

> Other aspects of work can give positive satisfaction.
> These are the <u>motivator factors</u>:
> <u>achievement</u> – the feeling that you have been successful in reaching your goals
> <u>recognition</u> – the feeling that your employers understand and value what you do by giving <u>positive feedback</u>
> <u>the work itself</u> – the nature and interest of the job
> <u>responsibility</u> – when you are in charge of something and its success or failure
> <u>advancement</u> – how far you will be promoted in the organization; how far you will go up the career ladder
> <u>personal growth</u> – how you develop personally in your work, and your opportunities to do this

## B Motivator factors

## C Empowerment

On the course, Yolanda also looked at a related but more recent idea.

> <u>Empowerment</u> – the idea that decisions, where possible, should be made by employees who are close to the issues or problems to be solved, without having to <u>consult</u> their managers further up in the <u>hierarchy</u>. In other words, managers have to <u>delegate</u> as much as possible.

[1] *Work and the Nature of Man* (Staples Press 1968)

**3.1** Look at the job advertisement. Match the circled items 1–6 to the hygiene factors in A opposite.

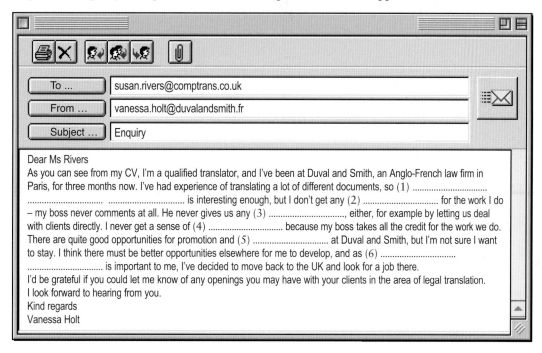

## Duval and Smith

**Legal Translator English-French**
**Paris** (1) €50,000
Large Anglo-French law firm seeks legal translator to translate and correct French and English legal documents. Legal qualifications and experience essential.
Based in the firm's busy translation department, you will work (2) under the head of translation, (3) as part of a team of five translators (4) In line with the overall policies of the firm you will work (5) a 35-hour week, with a (6) one-year contract in the first instance.

Email CV to jmartin@duvalandsmith.fr

**3.2** Vanessa Holt got the job advertised above. Three months later, she writes an email to an employment agency. Complete the email with expressions from B opposite.

To ... susan.rivers@comptrans.co.uk
From ... vanessa.holt@duvalandsmith.fr
Subject ... Enquiry

Dear Ms Rivers
As you can see from my CV, I'm a qualified translator, and I've been at Duval and Smith, an Anglo-French law firm in Paris, for three months now. I've had experience of translating a lot of different documents, so (1) ...............................
.............................. .............................. is interesting enough, but I don't get any (2) .............................. for the work I do – my boss never comments at all. He never gives us any (3) .............................., either, for example by letting us deal with clients directly. I never get a sense of (4) .............................. because my boss takes all the credit for the work we do. There are quite good opportunities for promotion and (5) .............................. at Duval and Smith, but I'm not sure I want to stay. I think there must be better opportunities elsewhere for me to develop, and as (6) ..............................
.............................. is important to me, I've decided to move back to the UK and look for a job there.
I'd be grateful if you could let me know of any openings you may have with your clients in the area of legal translation.
I look forward to hearing from you.
Kind regards
Vanessa Holt

**3.3** Complete the table with words from C opposite and related forms. Put a stress mark in front of the stressed syllable in each word. (The first one has been done for you.)

| Verb | Noun | Adjective |
|------|------|-----------|
| con'sult | consul'tation, con'sultancy con'sultant | con'sultative, con'sulting |
| delegate | | |
| empower | | |
| | | hierarchical |

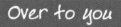

Talk or write to a new employee about your own organization or one you would like to work for, in relation to Herzberg's motivator factors.

# 4 Employment and employability

## Outsourcing

Nigel, a 30-year-old information technology (IT) specialist, talks about his career so far:

'I used to work in the IT department of a bank. All the IT work was done **in-house**. I thought I had a **job for life**. But then one day the bank decided to cut costs by **outsourcing** the work to a specialist IT company called IT Services (ITS).

Luckily, the bank didn't make me **redundant** so I didn't lose my job, and after a while I decided to work for ITS instead. At first, I didn't know what to expect, but now I'm very happy. We work with a lot of different clients – I'm a **consultant** and I give them advice.'

## B Employability

'ITS put a lot of emphasis on **professional development** and we often go on training courses so we can keep up with **current trends** in the industry.

ITS tell us that although we may not have a job for life with the company, our up-to-date skills will mean that we will always be **employable**. Companies and governments talk about the importance of **lifelong learning** – continuing to develop our knowledge by going on courses and reading journals, for example.

I really enjoy my work but in the next year or two, I may make a **career move** and join another company.'

## C Freelancers and portfolio workers

'When I'm about 40, I want to **set up on my own** as a **freelancer** offering **consultancy services** to different companies. The idea of working **freelance** on different projects for different clients attracts me.'

The management thinker Charles Handy[1] calls freelancers **portfolio workers** because they have a **portfolio** or range of different clients. Some experts say that increasing numbers of people will work this way in the future, as companies outsource more and more of their work because they want to concentrate on their **core functions**.

Note: People are called **freelancers** or **freelances**. The corresponding adjective is freelance, as in 'freelance work'.

[1] *The Age of Unreason* (Random House 2001)

**4.1** Complete the crossword with appropriate forms of expressions from A, B and C opposite.

**Across**

4 Training courses etc. related to work: .............. development. (12)

6 What many companies no longer offer. (3,3,4)

8 and 9 down  When you get a better job you make a .............. .............. . (6,4)

10 Someone who offers professional advice etc. to companies. (10)

11 Companies that buy in services from outside suppliers .............. these services. (9)

12 If you start work as a freelancer, you .............. .............. on your own. (3,2)

**Down**

1 Having the skills needed to get a job. (10)

2 and 3 Someone who does work for a number of different companies. (9,6)

5 The people in 2 and 3 down are also called .............. . (11)

7 If you lose your job, for example because it has been outsourced, you are made .............. . (9)

9 See 8 across.

**4.2** Complete the sentences with appropriate forms of expressions from A, B and C opposite. (There are two possibilities for one of the gaps.)

1 There's a lot to be said for ............................ ................................ . I would encourage more working men and women to refresh their skills on university short courses tailored to their needs. That way they can keep up with ............................ ................................ and make sure they are always aware of the latest thinking in their area.

2 I love my new job. This is definitely the best ............................ ................................ I could have made.

3 The company fired 11,000 employees and sold several business units. Non-core ............................ were outsourced.

4 Some former advertising executives offer ............................ ................................ to ad agencies, bringing expertise the agencies do not have themselves.

5 Some 'creative' businesses, like design services, have hardly any permanent staff and rely on work done by .............................. .

6 Of course, there are advantages to doing some things ............................-................................: you don't have to explain to outsiders what you want them to do.

**Over to you**

Would it be possible to do your job or one you would like as a freelancer? Why / Why not? What are the advantages and disadvantages of being a freelancer?

# 5 Flexibility and inflexibility

## A

### Ways of working

Nordland is an advanced industrialized country. In addition to outsourcing some functions to freelancers (see Unit 4), many organizations there are looking for ways of having more **flexible working**, for example:

- **temporary workers** who only work for short periods when they are needed, either on a **temporary contract** with a company, or through a **temp agency**
- **part-time workers** who work less than a full working week
- **job sharing**, where two people share a particular job, each of them working part-time.

## B Job flexibility

The government of Nordland is trying to encourage this kind of **job flexibility**, and it has passed laws that allow companies to **hire and fire** employees easily. When **letting people go**, companies only have to **give** them two weeks' **notice** and relatively small **redundancy payments**; one week's salary for every year worked is the norm.

The government has also reduced **unemployment benefits**, the money paid to people without jobs. They say that all these measures make for a **flexible job market** and encourage **job creation**. Critics say that this approach leads to **job insecurity**, with employers able to get rid of employees too easily.

## C Job protection

Sudonia is an advanced industrialized country with a very different approach. Companies in trouble are only allowed to **make employees redundant** after a long period of **consultation**. If employees are made redundant, they receive generous redundancy payments and then unemployment benefits. The government says people need this sort of **job protection**, and **trade unions** are fighting hard to keep it.

Payments to employees such as **sick pay**, and **parental leave** when they have time off following the birth of children, are also very generous. Mothers get 18 months' paid **maternity leave** and fathers get six months' **paternity leave**. But the **social charges** which employers and employees have to pay the government are very high.

> BrE: trade unions;
> AmE: labor unions

Critics say that this contributes to a **rigid labour market**, one with too much job protection. They say that this sort of **inflexibility** discourages job creation and leads in the long run to higher **unemployment** and slower **economic growth**. As a consequence, companies may look abroad for cheaper bases and workforces.

**5.1** Look at A opposite. Which type of work is each of these people referring to?

1 I work at the local council for two days a week, and my friend works in the same job on the other three days.

2 I work in a petrol station 20 hours a week.

3 I'm on a job at Clarkson's until the end of next week. Then I'll try and find something else.

**5.2** Melinda and Nigel, two managers from Sudonia, are talking about the issues in B and C opposite. Replace the underlined phrases with expressions with items from those sections. Pay attention to the grammatical context. (The first one has been done for you.)

Melinda: It's ridiculous! We can't <u>get rid of employees</u> without a lot of <u>meetings and discussion</u> with <u>employee organizations</u>, government officials and so on. We have to keep even the laziest, most incompetent people.

*We can't <u>make employees redundant</u> without a lot of <u>consultation</u> with <u>trade unions</u>, government officials and so on. We have to keep even the laziest, most incompetent people.*

Nigel: I know what you mean. I don't have the opportunity to <u>recruit and get rid of</u> people as I want! This sort of <u>rigidity</u> must be bad for the job market. <u>The number of people without jobs</u> in this country is very high.

Melinda: It's a nightmare! If you do want to get rid of people, you have to <u>tell them three months in advance</u>.

Nigel: Yes, and you should see the <u>amount of tax</u> I have to pay for each of my employees just so they can get <u>money when they fall ill</u>, and so on.

Melinda: We should move to Nordland, where they have a <u>job market that gives employers a lot of freedom</u>. The level of <u>new jobs being created</u> there is incredible. Sudonia should copy Nordland.

Nigel: I agree, but it never will, until it's too late!

**5.3** Look at the expressions in B and C opposite and say if these statements are true or false.

1 When companies let employees go, they make them redundant.
2 One person's job flexibility might be another's job insecurity.
3 In flexible job markets, hiring and firing is complex.
4 Employee benefits are paid for through social charges.
5 'Rigidity' is another word for 'inflexibility'.
6 When fathers take parental leave, this is called 'fatherly leave'.
7 The cost of job protection might be higher unemployment.

Over to you

Is your country more like Nordland or Sudonia? What are the advantages and disadvantages of flexible working?

# 6 Work-life balance

## Stress

People talk about being **under (a lot of) stress** or **pressure**. They say their work is **stressful** and that they feel **stressed** or **stressed out**. They want to find ways to **de-stress**. They may complain that they have **stress-related illness**. Some people may suffer **burn-out** or a complete **breakdown**, which means they are no longer able to work.

'Stress' often occurs in these combinations:

| stress | | |
|---|---|---|
| | factor | something that causes stress |
| | symptom | a sign that someone is under stress |
| | toll | the total amount of damage caused by stress |
| | management | ways of dealing with stress |
| | industry | term used by critics to refer to counselling, research, etc. done in relation to stress |

Note: 'Stress' and 'pressure' are both countable and uncountable: you can also talk about the stresses and pressures you are under.

## B The causes of stress

The most common causes of stress are:

- **heavy workloads:** too much to do in the limited time available
- **office politics:** problems with colleagues who above all, want to advance their own position. These people like **playing politics**
- **role ambiguity:** responsibilities are unclear
- lack of **management support:** managers do not provide the necessary help and resources
- **effort-reward imbalance:** not getting sufficient recognition or pay
- **home-work imbalance:** not enough time for family, personal interests, etc.

## C Quality of life

Some people are **workaholics** – they think about very little except work. Others are increasingly looking for **quality of life**: less commuting, more time with their families, etc. Journalists write about people **downshifting** or **rebalancing** their lives. They may work part-time, work from home, move to the country and so on.

In a recent survey:

a  95 per cent of **homeworkers** said they have a better **work-life balance** or **home-work balance** than when they were in-company because they can spend more time with their families and on leisure activities.

b  82 per cent said they have more **autonomy** and **independence**: they are able to organize their work and their time how they want.

But in the same survey homeworkers also complained that:

c  there is no **boundary** between work on the one hand and personal life on the other – the two **overlap** (73 per cent)

d  they feel lonely and **isolated** because they are out of contact with others and don't have colleagues around them (57 per cent).

**6.1** Complete the article with appropriate forms of 'stress' from A opposite.

# Payouts predicted for stressed teachers

Teachers could win settlements of up to £250,000 over work-related (1) ............................., a senior lawyer for the National Union of Teachers has predicted, following last week's £47,000 compensation deal for a Wirral secondary teacher made ill by overwork.

For those who believe that teaching is an easy life, the story of Muriel Benson came as a reminder of the pressures. She was forced to retire three years ago from a senior post at Prenton High School because her health could not stand up to a 66-hour weekly workload.

Wirral council is refusing to discuss Benson's case, but, according to her side of the story, the breakdown that led to her early retirement also followed a failure by her employers to address the problems causing her (2) ............................. illness.

Doug McAvoy, the general secretary of the National Union of Teachers, said: "This case is clearly a warning to teachers' employers that neglect of a (3) ............................. situation could lead to significant medical damage. They must not allow that danger to develop and destroy a teacher's career. We know there are hundreds of teachers out there who are feeling (4) ............................. and pressured. They can be protected if they come to us for help."

But Neil Fletcher, education secretary of the Local Government Association, said: "There is no evidence that teaching is becoming more (5) ............................. ."

*The Guardian*

**6.2** Which two of the causes of stress in B opposite are specifically mentioned in the article above?

**6.3** Match the statements (1–4) to the findings in the survey in C opposite.

1 Sometimes I wish I was working every day as part of a team in an office.

2 Yes, I see much more of my children.

3 Yes, my boss isn't breathing down my neck the whole time.

4 I work in the living room, and the work is always there, waiting. I can't get away from it.

## Over to you

Look again at the article above. Do you think that working 66 hours a week is always stressful? Why / Why not?

What are the main causes of stress in your job or one you would like? How do you combat stress?

# 7 Managing talent

## A Core competents

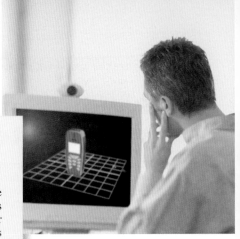

### Devising strategies to prevent the flight of talent

Is your company today held dependent on **"core competents"** – talented individuals possessing the skills that make your products and services unique? If so, you're not alone. In a study by the Corporate Leadership Council, a computer company recognised 100 core competents out of 16,000 employees; a software company had 10 out of 11,000; and a transportation group deemed 20 of its 33,000 employees truly **critical** to performance.

Core competents will stay only as long as organisations can offer them something they desire. Bear in mind, though, that this phenomenon concerns a small group of highly skilled people. However, **talent** does not necessarily equate to an impressive title. Core competents need not be senior executives, but could just as easily be people whose **intellectual property** is crucial to the organisation, or whose particular **expertise** is difficult to replicate.

No company ever went bankrupt because it suffered from having too much talent. Recent research shows that only 7 per cent of all managers strongly agree with the statement "our company has enough talented managers to pursue all or most of its promising opportunities".

In addition, 75 per cent of executives worldwide now rank **human performance** ahead of productivity and technology in terms of strategic importance. The same study also reveals that 80 per cent of all executives claim that by 2010 **attracting** and **retaining** people will be the leading success factor in strategy.

*Financial Times*

## B Creatives and suits

An expert in workplace trends says:

'Some activities depend on groups of freelance **creatives** for each project. For example, in film-making, the creatives, that is, the writers, director, etc., and the **talent** – the actors – come together for a particular project and then **disband**. This is a typical example of a **virtual organization**. The only permanent people in the company are the **suits**, the businesspeople, who bring the teams together for each project. Other industries work in similar ways.

For example, in software development, managers and programmers may come together to contribute to a particular project and then leave to work on others.'

Note: 'Suits' is mostly used in the plural and is colloquial.

**7.1** Look at the article in A opposite and say if these statements are true or false.
Core competents …

1 are highly skilled people.
2 are key to the functioning of some organizations.
3 are always senior executives.
4 have knowledge that is easy for other people to acquire.
5 are in plentiful supply
6 and the way they work is thought to be more important than at least two other factors in a company's success.
7 will be important for companies to recruit and keep in the future.

**7.2** Complete the sentences with expressions from A opposite.

1 Core competents are employees who have been identified as ............................. to the success of the company.

2 People who have specialized knowledge or ............................. are very valuable to the company.

3 Some say that people are a firm's most important assets, and therefore .............................
............................. is key to its success.

4 For many hi-tech companies, ............................. ............................. is their most important asset, more important than their physical assets.

5 The problem with ............................. is that it can just walk out of the door – we have to find ways of ............................. it initially, and then ............................. it so that it doesn't go to competitors.

6 In fact, getting the best out of ............................. ............................. is the most important skill these days for many managers.

**7.3** Look at B opposite. In a film project, are each of the following people 'creatives' or 'suits'?

1 the film director
2 the finance director
3 the actors
4 the head of the film company
5 the scriptwriter
6 the costume designers

## Over to you

Who are the core competents in your organization or one you would like to work for?
Why are they critical?

# 8 Team building

## A Teams

In some (but not all) situations, tasks can be achieved more easily by **teams** with a **common purpose**, rather than by individuals. Of course, it's important to develop **team work** through **team building** so as to get the best from the team.

## B Team players

Meredith Belbin[1] has identified these types of team members or **team players**:

a the **implementer**, who converts the team's plan into something achievable

b the **co-ordinator**, a confident member who sets objectives and defines team members' roles

c the **shaper**, who defines issues, shapes ideas and leads the action

d the **plant**, a creative and imaginative person who supplies original ideas and solves problems

e the **resource investigator**, who communicates with the outside world and explores opportunities

f the **monitor evaluator**, who sees all the possibilities, evaluates situations objectively, and sees what is realistically achievable

g the **teamworker**, who builds the team, supports others and reduces conflict

h the **completer**, who meets deadlines, corrects mistakes and makes sure nothing is forgotten.

## C Stages of team life

The typical team goes through a series of stages:

a **forming**: the group is anxious and feels dependent on a leader; the group tries to discover how it is going to operate and what the 'normal' ways of working will be

b **storming**: the atmosphere may be one of conflict between members, who may resist control from any one person; there may be the feeling that the task cannot be achieved

c **norming**: at this stage, members of the group feel closer together and the conflicts are forgotten; members of the group will start to support each other; there is increasingly the feeling that it is possible to achieve the task

d **performing**: the group is carrying out the task for which it was formed; members feel safe enough to express differences of opinion in relation to others

e **mourning**: the group's work is finished, and its members begin to have pleasant memories of their activities and achievements.

[1] *Management Teams: Why They Succeed or Fail* (Butterworth–Heinemann 1996)

8.1 Look at the types of team members in B opposite and say if these statements are true or false.

1 Implementers are not interested in final results.
2 Co-ordinators tend to take a leading, organizing role.
3 Shapers tend to follow what other people say.
4 Plants can be useful in providing new ideas when the team has run out of steam.
5 Some resource investigators might love using the Internet.
6 Monitor evaluators are not good at seeing all sides of a problem.
7 Teamworkers may help to defuse arguments between members.
8 Completers are bad at finishing things on time.

8.2 Members of a team brought together to work on a design project said the following things. Match them to the stages in C opposite. (There are two sentences relating to each stage.)

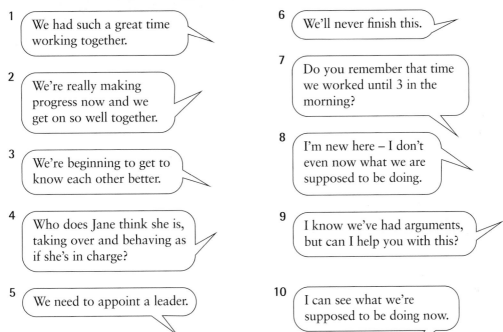

1 We had such a great time working together.

2 We're really making progress now and we get on so well together.

3 We're beginning to get to know each other better.

4 Who does Jane think she is, taking over and behaving as if she's in charge?

5 We need to appoint a leader.

6 We'll never finish this.

7 Do you remember that time we worked until 3 in the morning?

8 I'm new here – I don't even now what we are supposed to be doing.

9 I know we've had arguments, but can I help you with this?

10 I can see what we're supposed to be doing now.

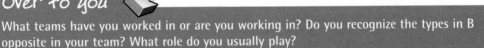

## Over to you

What teams have you worked in or are you working in? Do you recognize the types in B opposite in your team? What role do you usually play?

# 9 The right skills

## A Hard and soft skills

For a long time, **hard skills**, for example skills in technical subjects, were considered the most important thing in business. But more and more, people are realizing the importance of **soft skills** – the skills you need to work with other people, and in the case of managers, to manage people in **tactful** and **non-authoritarian, non-dictatorial** ways.

## B Emotional intelligence

### You've got the brains but have you got the touch?

While IQ has traditionally been the means by which we judge someone's abilities and potential, **EQ** – the E stands for emotional – is the new benchmark for a new world. If you've got it, you're more likely to be powerful, successful and have fulfilling relationships than if you haven't. **Emotional intelligence** – the ability to understand and control your emotions, and recognize and respond to those of others – is emerging as the single most important and effective business and personal skill of the new century.

At American Express, financial advisers who'd been through emotional intelligence training improved sales by up to 20 per cent, significantly more than the company average. A ten-year study by Sheffield University of over 100 small- and medium-sized UK businesses found that **people management** was three times as important as research and development in improving productivity and profitability and six times as important as business strategy.

Daniel Goleman, a US science journalist-turned-consultant with a background in psychology, first popularized the notion of emotional intelligence in the mid-nineties. Goleman defines five elements of emotional intelligence: **self-awareness, self-regulation, motivation, empathy** and **social skills**. Sceptics argue that this sounds suspiciously like the old **soft skills**, in management-course speak, dressed up in new clothing. But Tim Sparrow, of human performance consultants Buckholdt Associates, points out a crucial difference. 'Soft skills training was only about **interpersonal intelligence** – relating to others. Emotional intelligence involves intrapersonal skills – knowing yourself – as well. You can't be **interpersonally** intelligent if you don't recognise feelings in yourself.'

*The Observer*

**9.1** Look at A opposite. Were (a) hard skills or (b) soft skills mainly required at each of the following stages of a project to design insurance products? The project manager ...

1 employed someone with a doctorate in mathematics to work on risk probabilities.
2 gave three days off to a team member who said they had family problems at home.
3 analyzed her own feelings of frustration that the project was going too slowly.
4 dealt politely but firmly with a request by her boss to finish the project a month early.
5 did market testing of the product with a number of potential consumers of the product and analyzed the results on computer.
6 did careful research on the Internet to find the best advertising agency to launch the product.

**9.2** Complete the sentences with appropriate forms of expressions from B opposite.

1 If someone is good at persuading employees to do things without making them annoyed, they are good at .............................. .............................. .

2 More generally, getting along with people and avoiding tactless remarks are examples of
.............................. .............................. .

3 Knowing your own emotions and feelings is ..............................-.............................. : this is an
.............................. skill.  Contrast this with the ability to get along with other people: ..............................
skills.

4 If you are able to control your own emotions, you have good ..............................-.............................. .

5 If you are able to understand how other people feel, you have .............................. with them.

6 The whole area is referred to by Daniel Goleman as .............................. .............................. . The abbreviation for the way this is measured is .............................. .

**9.3** Find the words and phrases (1–6) in the article in B opposite and match them to their meanings (a–f).

| | |
|---|---|
| 1 benchmark | a (gradually) becoming |
| 2 fulfilling | b a reference point by which you judge something |
| 3 emerging as | c terminology from a management course |
| 4 sceptics | d given a new image |
| 5 management-course speak | e making you feel happy and satisfied |
| 6 dressed up in new clothing | f people who doubt the truth of an idea |

### Over to you

Write a description of the soft skills required for your job or one you would like.

## A Defining quality

### Staying in the lead means continually raising the bar

In 1980, a television documentary in the US entitled *If Japan Can, Why Can't We?* announced that it had discovered the secret of Japanese competitive success: quality. Japanese companies were successfully dominating world markets because they had a **quality system** that allowed them to produce better products than their US rivals.

What was more, the documentary said, the Japanese had learned this quality system from US experts such as W Edwards Deming and Joseph Juran. What US and other western businesses had to do now was relearn the techniques of **quality management**.

The central problem revolves around an understanding of what 'quality' is and how far the concept can be applied across the organisation. Definitions can vary, but it is generally accepted that the three elements which constitute quality are **fitness of the design**, **conformity to specification** and **satisfying customer needs**.

Today, quality is most often defined by the reaction of the customer who buys and uses the product. If the customer is satisfied, so the theory goes, the product is of sufficient quality. However, a strategy based on no more than meeting customer expectations is a dangerous one, as it opens the door to rivals that may produce better products.

*Financial Times*

Note: **Specifications** are referred to informally as **specs**.

## B Quality in manufacturing

Gordon Greer is head of quality at a car component company:

'The design for each component embodies the intentions of its designer. So conformity to specification means putting these intentions into practice when we make the components.
Put another way, this is **elimination of variation**.

We pay great attention to **accuracy**. The components must be made to very strict **tolerances** – the measurements must be not more or less than particular limits to within a fraction of a millimetre.'

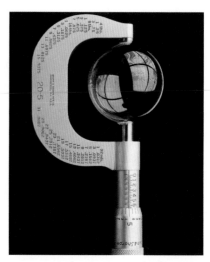

A micrometer

## C Quality in services

Serena Togliatti is customer relations manager at a large bank:

'In services, there is a parallel situation to the one in manufacturing. The service received by the customer must be exactly what is planned and intended, and annoying mistakes, for example in their accounts, must be avoided.

From the customer's point of view, quality could be defined in terms of **customer approval,** that is, recognition that we are satisfying customer needs and **customer expectations**. And if we exceed those expectations, there may even be **customer delight**.' (See Unit 23)

**10.1** Look at A and B opposite and answer the questions.
Which expression refers to:

1 the idea of following a designer's intentions?
2 the work of making sure that the principles of quality are applied?
3 approaching quality in a logical way?
4 keeping customers happy?
5 how good a design is for the purpose of the product it relates to?

**10.2** Complete the table with words from A, B and C opposite and related forms. Put a stress mark in front of the stressed syllable in each word of more than one syllable. (The first one has been done for you.)

| Verb | Noun |
|---|---|
| a'pprove (of) | a'pproval |
| conform (to) | |
| | delight |
| eliminate | |
| expect | |
| fit | |
| | satisfaction |
| specify | |
| | tolerance |
| vary | |

Now use correct forms of the expressions above and opposite to replace the underlined words and phrases in this memo from the head of a package holiday company.

Memo                     **CLUB SOLEIL**

From: Jacqueline Toubon

To: All hotel managers

Buying a family holiday is a big investment for a lot of people, both financially and emotion-ally. So, we don't just want (1) <u>them to be happy with what they get</u>; we want (2) <u>them to be extremely happy</u>.

We want to avoid the situation where things are different from what customers were expect-ing and instead we want (3) <u>standards to be exactly as described</u>. When the hotel does not come up to the description in the brochure, our clients are extremely angry.
This means (4) <u>avoiding changes or differences</u> in relation to what we promise.

Customers may find that things are better than they thought they would be, for example, the food may be better or the rooms more comfortable. Although this may be a way of going beyond (5) <u>what customers were hoping for</u>, it is important to keep control of costs. To use a comparison with manufacturing industry, we have to keep standards within certain (6) <u>limits</u>.

*Over to you*

What are the criteria for quality in your organization or one you would like to work for?

# 11 Quality standards

## A Standards and certification

*The ISO is the registered trademark of the International Organization for Standardization and is reproduced here by kind permission of ISO.*

The **International Organization for Standardization** is based in Geneva. It is a network of national **standards institutes** from over 145 countries working in partnership with international organizations, governments, industry, business and consumer representatives.

ISO has developed more than 14,000 International **Standards**, which it says are "documented agreements containing **technical specifications** or other precise **criteria** and **guidelines** to ensure that materials, products, processes and services are **fit for their purpose**".

There are two series of standards for management systems: the ISO 9000 series on quality management and the ISO 14000 series on environmental management. Organizations can **apply for certification** to ISO 9001:2000 and ISO 14001:1996. (For more on environmental standards, see Unit 43.)

Note: Singular: **criterion**, plural: **criteria**

## B ISO 9000

The 2000 version of the ISO 9000 standards put particular importance on:

a the role of **top management** in setting policies for quality

Top managers have to be seen to be involved in quality issues, not leaving this to middle management

b **statutory** and **regulatory requirements** – for example, the car industry has to pay particular attention to safety and environmental laws and standards in relation to the components that they use

c **measurable objectives** – we have to be able to measure quality and by how much it is improving

d **resource management** – how we manage the <u>inputs</u> to our products, for example in <u>human resources</u> and <u>materials</u>

e monitoring **customer satisfaction** – customers are the ultimate judges of quality and we have to constantly check and improve the 'score' that they give us

f **training effectiveness** – the training of our staff is an investment and we have to measure how effective it is in terms of our future profitability

g **continual improvement** – 100 per cent quality is never achieved – there is always room for improvement. (See Unit 12)

**11.1** Complete the table with words from A opposite. Put a stress mark in front of the stressed syllable in each word. (The first one has been done for you.)

| | Verb | Noun | Adjective |
|---|---|---|---|
| 1 | 'certify/certifi'cate | cert'ificate/certific'ation | 'certified/cert'ificated |
| 2 | apply | | |
| 3 | | standard/standardization | |

Now complete each sentence (1–3) with the correct form of the word from the table with the same number.

1 ISO .............................. will give us more credibility with our clients and so we've asked to be .............................. by them.

2 They told us to bring in ISO-approved consultants to check our operations and make our .............................. through them.

3 Now we can put the ISO 9000 logo on all our literature. We've .............................. all our documentation so that it's clearly visible. Our clients feel reassured – in fact, they love it!

**11.2** Look at these examples of work on quality at a company producing car components. Match each one to an aspect of quality (a–g) in B opposite.

1 All the people in the call centre were sent on a course to develop their sense of team work, and this increased sales by 15 per cent.

2 The senior managers invited a well-known quality expert to do a consultancy project on production quality.

3 The production manager looked at the latest regulations on car safety on a government Ministry of Transport website.

4 Employees are always paid bonuses for suggesting improvements, however small.

5 The company developed new software to analyze quality data more closely.

6 They have checked the quality procedures in place at all of their suppliers.

7 The car firms who buy the company's components are totally satisfied.

A call centre

Over to you

Find out about an organization (perhaps your own or one of its suppliers) that has adopted standards such as ISO 9000. How have they changed the way that the company works?

# 12 TQM and JIT

## A Total quality management

**Total quality management,** or **TQM,** was fashionable in the 1980s. This often involved **quality circles,** groups of workers who were encouraged to contribute ideas on improving the products that they made. Some companies had quality circles of production workers who suggested better ways of organizing the **production line.**

**Employee participation,** for example getting employees to suggest improvements to production methods, as in total quality management, is a form of **empowerment:** employees **have a voice** in quality improvements, rather than just following managers' instructions. (See Units 2 and 3)

## B Kaizen

The TQM approach was designed to bring about gradual, step-by-step or **incremental improvements** in quality. **Continuous improvement** is what the Japanese call **kaizen.** An essential part of kaizen is **gemba** – 'the place where things happen'. In manufacturing, this is, of course, the factory floor. The idea is that continuous improvements can best be made by the people directly involved with production.

*Kaizen*

## C Just-in-time production

Originating in Japan, and then adopted all over the industrialized world, TQM forms part of **lean production,** making things with the minimum of time, effort and materials. Instead of producing components in large **batches,** they are delivered or produced **just in time (JIT),** only as they are needed. Employees are empowered to correct problems on the spot. Things must be done **right first time (RFT).** There should be no **reworking** to correct **defects** on finished products.

Production is seen as a continuous **process** of sequential rather than isolated steps, and the **production,** or **assembly line** is laid out in a logical way. Stocks of components are kept to a minimum. Manufacturing organized in steps like this is **flow production.**

*A modern production line*

**12.1** Complete the crossword with appropriate forms of expressions from A, B and C opposite.

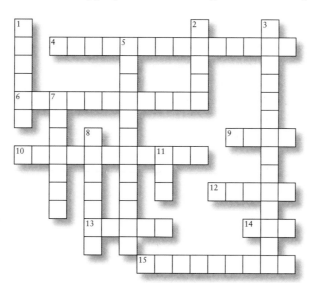

**Across**

4  Groups of improving workers. (7,7)
6  Handing responsibility to people lower down the organization. (11)
9  .............. production is done in series of stages. (4)
10  and 5 down  When things get gradually better. (11,12)
12  A group of identical things produced. (5)
13  When quality is absolute. (5)
14  Abbreviation for when things are made as they are needed. (1,1,1)
15  The aim of RFT is to avoid .............. . (9)

**Down**

1  Japanese for continuous improvement. (6)
2  Avoid reworking: get it .............. first time. (5)
3  Making things with the minimum of resources. (4,10)
5  See 10 across.
7  All production activities seen as a whole. (7)
8  Errors and problems. (7)
11  Abbreviation for the methods used when quality is the main goal. (1,1,1)

**12.2** What aspects of Quality Management are these employees talking about? Complete the sentences, with expressions from A, B and C opposite.

1  'Our bosses encourage us to make suggestions about improving the production process if it's good for quality. We have a high level of ................................ .................................. .'
2  'We feel that we ................................ .................................. .................................. and that we are listened to.'
3  'Do it ................................ .................................. .................................. and you don't have to do it again.'
4  'Products being worked on move a minimum distance to the next step in the production process. This ................................ .................................. means there is minimum time lost between each step.'

## Over to you

Do you think it's always possible to go on improving quality incrementally, or can you reach a state where it is so good that further improvement is impossible?

# 13 Quality and people

## A Investors in people

There are **models** and **frameworks** that emphasize the human dimension in improving quality.

**Investors in People** is a framework developed in the UK. It sets a level of **good practice** for training and development of people to achieve business goals.

The **Investors in People Standard** is based on four key principles:

a **Commitment** to invest in people to achieve business goals

b **Planning** how skills, individuals and teams are to be developed to achieve these goals

c **Action** to develop and use necessary skills in a well defined and continuing programme directly tied to business objectives

d **Evaluating outcomes**, the results of training and development for individuals' progress towards their goals and the goals of the organization as a whole.

## B The EFQM Excellence Model

The **EFQM Excellence Model** was developed by the European Foundation for Quality Management, a non-profit organization set up by leading European companies to 'help European businesses make better products and deliver improved services through the effective use of leading edge management practices'.

In this model, people are very much part of the wider quality picture. It refers to company **stakeholders,** who are not only its employees, shareholders and customers but also the community as a whole.

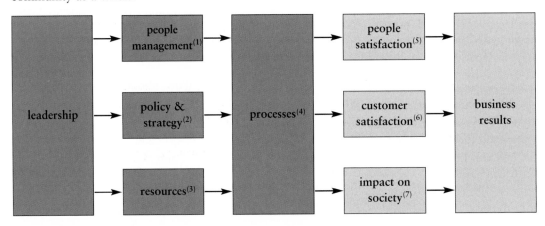

**13.1** A firm decided to introduce Investors in People principles. Look at the reports from the management and match them to the four principles in A opposite. (There are two statements relating to each principle.)

1 We've set up a committee of managers to work on the planning of skills development for individuals and teams in their departments.

5 They asked groups of employees to contribute ideas on ways of improving their skills.

2 We've announced in the internal company newspaper that we are going to apply the principles.

6 I've asked all our managers to report verbally on the progress of their employees in working towards the goals.

3 We've asked external consultants to quantify financially the effectiveness of the actions they had undertaken.

7 I was sent on a training course with the other managers. We learned how to improve our management techniques.

4 They sent all employees on a three-day quality training course.

8 We've announced on our customer website that we're going to apply the Investors in People principles.

**13.2** Match the two parts of the descriptions below relating to the EFQM Excellence model in B opposite. (The numbers on the left relate to those in the model.)

Excellent organisations…

1 manage their people at all levels in order to

2 develop a stakeholder focused strategy which takes account of the market in order to

3 plan and manage external partnerships and internal resources in order to

4 design, manage and improve processes in order to

5, 6, 7 comprehensively measure their performance in order to

a fully satisfy and generate increasing value for customers and other stakeholders.

b support policy and strategy.

c develop their full potential.

d achieve outstanding results with their people and with respect to their customers and to society in general.

e implement their mission.

Over to you

Find out about an organization and describe it in terms of the EFQM framework.

# 14 The management of change

Business process re-engineering

In the 1990s, **business process re-engineering**, or **BPR**, emerged. Inspired by a book by Michael Hammer and James Champy[1], consultants told companies not to bother with incremental improvements, but to abolish everything, **go back to the drawing board** and **redesign** all the business processes involved in producing something, whether a product or a service. They said that this redesign should be:

- **fundamental:** asking basic questions about what a process is meant to achieve
- **radical:** going to the root of things and ignoring completely how things were done before, 'like starting again with a new sheet of paper'
- **dramatic:** bringing about very big and sudden changes.

In the eyes of critics, BPR often meant **delayering** – removing **management layers**, perhaps resulting in **job losses**.

## B The benefits of BPR

For its supporters, these are some of the strengths of BPR:

a **leadership:** strong leadership is important; changes are imposed from above; there is visible **commitment** from leaders for change

b **people management:** fewer **management layers** mean larger, more challenging jobs

c **policy and strategy:** clearer **fit** between the organization and its declared purpose and goals

d **processes:** managers and employees gain improved awareness and understanding of key processes

e **customer satisfaction:** clear **focus** of processes on the customer for existing products and services

f **business results:** dramatic improvements for companies in crisis.

(The headings are from the EFQM Model – see Unit 13)

[1] *Re-engineering the Corporation: A Manifesto for Business Revolution* (Nicholas Brealey 2001)

**14.1** Gordon Greer, production manager at a car components manufacturer (see Unit 10) is talking about a car company that he supplies called Autoco. Replace the underlined words and phrases with expressions from A opposite. Pay attention to the grammatical context.

'One example of (1) <u>restructuring</u> that I know was quite (2) <u>basic</u>: Autoco, one of our customers, wanted to simplify its supplier payments system.

Before, there were three documents relating to every delivery. We got a purchase order from Autoco, a delivery note accompanied the goods when they were delivered to them, and then we sent an invoice. There were 300 employees in their accounts department. Within the department there were sub-departments, each dealing with payments for different groups of suppliers, and each with its own head.

The accounts payable department at Autoco checked that copies of the three documents matched before making payment – there were often problems with documents, and this delayed payment, which caused us problems.

Autoco made a (3) <u>very big and sudden</u> change, one that was (4) <u>designed to go to the root of things</u>. When goods were received, this was entered on Autoco's computer system, and the goods were paid for automatically – we no longer had to send invoices, and were paid promptly.

The number of people in the accounts payable department at Autoco was reduced to 15. There was (5) <u>a reduction in the number of management layers</u> as the sub-department heads were no longer needed, but the company was expanding elsewhere, and the people who were no longer needed were given new jobs within the company, so there were no (6) <u>employees made redundant</u>.'

**14.2** Look at these criticisms (1–6) that have been made of BPR. Match each criticism to one of its claimed benefits (a–f) in B opposite.

1 Results may be harmed by the chaos and confusion that BPR brings to the organization.
2 People can be left demotivated and demoralized by radical change.
3 Smooth, gradual, incremental introduction of completely new processes is not possible.
4 If the company is in crisis, there can be a tendency to concentrate too much on the internal workings of the organization and lose sight of the actions of competitors, and the success/failure of the organization's strategy.
5 The need for BPR implies bad earlier management, but the existing senior managers hardly ever want to re-engineer themselves out of a job.
6 There can be a tendency to concentrate too much on the existing products/services of the organization, ignoring new customer needs.

### Over to you
You have been asked by the mayor of your town or city to re-engineer one of its services. Which service most needs improving? How would you restructure it? (Money is no obstacle!)

# 15 Striving for perfection

## Benchmarking and best practice

**Benchmarking** is the idea that a firm should find out which company performs a particular task best and model its **performance** on this **best practice**. Companies talk about carrying out a **benchmarking exercise**. To do this, they **benchmark themselves against** other companies.

Large companies can measure the performance of different departments in relation to each other in an **internal benchmarking** exercise. **Competitive benchmarking** involves looking outside the company at how other companies in the same industry do things.

**Functional benchmarking** looks at how the same function such as manufacturing or personnel recruitment is done by non-competitors. Companies can learn a lot from firms who are not their direct competitors. For example, a train company has learned how to organize the cleaning of its trains better by looking at how an airline organizes the cleaning of its planes.

One way of seeing how a competitor's product is made is by **reverse engineering** – taking the product apart to see how it is made. The same principle can also be applied to services. This technique can also be used in benchmarking.

Note: 'Best practice' is usually uncountable, but you can also talk about 'the best practices' in a particular area.

## Six sigma quality

Quality can be measured in terms of the number of **defects per million** parts, operations, etc. For example, **one sigma** equals 690,000 defects per million parts and two sigma means 45,000 defects per million. Even with **two sigma quality**, the chances of a manufactured product being defective are quite high.

Motorola was the first company to aim for **six sigma quality**. In manufacturing, six sigma quality is when there are fewer than 3.4 defects per million components. This idea can also be applied in areas outside manufacturing. In invoicing, for example, it means fewer than three or four mistakes per million transactions.

**Six sigma quality** has been taken up by several other companies.

And the ultimate goal is **zero defects** – no defects at all.

**15.1** Complete the sentences with appropriate forms of expressions from A opposite.

1 The manufacturers' association wants companies to improve manufacturing .............. , so it's offering a new service designed to help companies .............. themselves against the best in their industries.

2 Engineers made replacement parts for the cars by copying the shape and dimensions of the original parts, a process known as .............. .............. .

3 Internal .............. looks for internal .............. .............. and tries to establish them throughout the organization.

4 We use .............. .............. to evaluate the effectiveness of your website against those of your competitors.

5 Look outside your industry! .............. .............. can teach you a lot, and as the companies you are asking to give you advice are not your competitors, they may be more willing to help.

**15.2** Read the article relating to the ideas in B opposite. Then answer 'yes' or 'no' to the questions below about the vocabulary used in the article.

---

# When quality is not enough

Quality improvement programmes come in many different flavours. The most common are Total Quality Management (TQM), Six Sigma and the Baldrige system promoted by the government-backed National Institute of Standards and Technology (NIST).

There are more similarities than differences between them. The common belief is that companies should aim for 'zero defects' in all aspects of their operations, achieved by relentless improvements in business processes. Common techniques include a team-based approach to problem-solving and a highly quantitative approach to measuring results.

Motorola, maker of microprocessors and cellphones, developed Six Sigma as a technique to improve the competitiveness of its manufacturing. The aim of the strategy is to reduce defects to fewer than 3.4 for every million repetitions of any process. But despite achieving Six Sigma quality in many areas of its business – and being the first large company to win a Baldrige quality award from the NIST – Motorola has often struggled. It is now engaged in a painful restructuring programme.

Given this mixed experience, why are many US companies now adopting Six Sigma? Fashion and the influence of General Electric are big factors. Jack Welch, GE's recently retired chairman and chief executive, was introduced to Six Sigma in the mid-1990s by Larry Bossidy, a former GE colleague who at the time was running Allied Signal. Mr Bossidy had, in turn, picked up the idea from Motorola, with which Allied Signal did business.

Quality was at the time an unfashionable management concept. The TQM fad of the 1980s had run out of steam. Received wisdom was that more radical approaches such as business process re-engineering were required if companies were to stay competitive.

Undeterred, in 1996 Mr Welch declared Six Sigma quality to be his next group-wide initiative for GE. By the end of the decade he was declaring it a spectacular success: his 1999 letter to shareholders attributed '$2bn in benefits' to the Six Sigma programme.

*Financial Times*

---

1 If something is *promoted* by a particular organization, does it have that organization's support?

2 If improvements are *relentless*, do they keep on happening?

3 Does a *quantitative* approach to something depend on general descriptions and feelings about it?

4 If restructuring is *painful*, is it easy?

5 If an organization *adopts* an approach, does it accept it and use it?

6 Do *former* colleagues still work together?

7 Is a *fad* a genuine and important change that will last?

8 If a movement *runs out of steam*, does it continue and develop?

9 Is a *spectacular* success a very big one?

---

Over to you

Think about your organization or one you would like to work for. How much do you know about how its competitors do things? Do you think it's useful to know how effective they are in different areas?

# 16 Strategic thinking

## Strategy

A **strategy** (countable noun) is a plan or series of plans for achieving success. **Strategy** (uncountable noun) is the study of the skills, knowledge, etc. required to make such plans. **Strategic** success in a commercial organization is often measured in terms of **profitability**, the amount of money it makes in relation to the amount invested.

An important part of **planning** is **resource allocation**. This is the way finance, people and **assets** – equipment, buildings, know-how, etc. – are going to be used to achieve a particular **objective**.

A company's senior executives make **strategic decisions** or **formulate strategy**. Sometimes an organisation will publicly state its main overall objective or **vision** in its **mission statement**.

Companies sometimes form **strategic partnerships,** working together to achieve a specific **strategic goal**. For example, MG Rover entered a partnership with a Chinese car manufacturer to enable it to produce and sell cars in China. A company may also make a **strategic move**, such as acquiring a competitor, designed to increase their market share.

## B Companies and markets

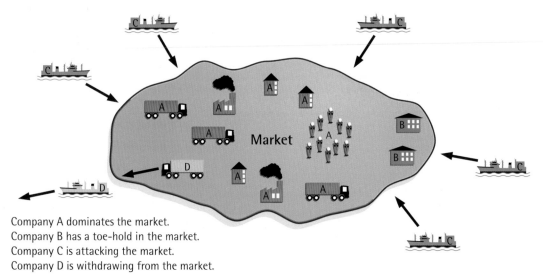

Company A dominates the market.
Company B has a toe-hold in the market.
Company C is attacking the market.
Company D is withdrawing from the market.

| When a company ... | | |
|---|---|---|
| a **defends** | | tries to prevent competitors from being successful in it. |
| b **attacks** | | starts selling in it for the first time. |
| c **establishes a foothold/ toehold in** | a market, it | occupies a small part of it first in preparation for gaining a larger part. |
| d **invades** | | starts to be very successful in it. |
| e **dominates** | | is the biggest competitor in it. |
| f **withdraws from** | | stops selling in it. |

**16.1** Look at the questions from shareholders at the annual meeting of Topaz, a car company. Complete the chief executive's answers with appropriate forms of expressions from A opposite.

1
> Why has the company bought out its rival, Rivera?

> This was a .............................. .............................. to broaden our customer base.

2
> Some of Topaz's plants have very low productivity. What are you doing about this?

> We have taken steps to ensure that our .............................. are used more effectively. This is an important part of our strategic .............................. process.

3
> Why are you closing one of the plants?

> This is an issue of .............................. .............................. . We don't have infinite financial resources and we want to concentrate investment on the most productive plants.

4
> Was this the only goal that was considered? Did you also look at the possibility of being a mass producer of vehicles?

> We looked at a number of different .............................. and decided that the hi-tech option was the best one to follow.

**16.2** Match the underlined phrases below to the expressions in B opposite that refer to the same idea.

Coffeeway (CW) is a successful American chain of coffee shops. It wanted to (1) aggressively enter the Chinese coffee shop market, with shops all over China. CW signed an agreement with a partner, Dragon Enterprises (DE). CW and DE decided to (2) start by opening just one coffee shop in Shanghai in order to test the market. This was very successful, so CW and DE decided to open shops all over China. It took CW and DE five years to (3) be the biggest in the market, with a 70 per cent market share among coffee shop chains in China. One of their competitors, California Coffee, tried to (4) protect its market share by cutting prices. But this strategy did not work, and California Coffee later sold its outlets to CW/DE and decided to (5) leave the market.

## Over to you

Think about your organization or one you would like to work for. Look at its website and find its mission statement. If it doesn't have one, what would you suggest?

# 17 Competition

## Competitors

The main competitors in a particular industry are its **key players**. Smaller competitors may be referred to as **minor players**.

**Competition** in an industry can be:

- cut-throat
- intense
- keen
- stiff
- ferocious
- fierce
- low-key
- tough

The usual pattern for a new industry is to have a large number of competitors: there may be **start-ups** – completely new companies – and there may be companies already **established** in other **sectors** that also want to **get into the industry,** perhaps by setting up a new **subsidiary** or **business unit**. (See Unit 19)

## 'Competing' and 'competitive'

**Competing** and **competitive** are adjectives related to 'competition'. Two companies may produce **competing products** – products that compete with each other. A **competitive product** is one that has real and specific benefits in relation to others of the same type.

'Competing' also occurs in these combinations:

| competing | | |
|---|---|---|
| | **bids** | price offers for a company in a takeover |
| | **offerings** | products from different companies |
| | **suppliers** | companies offering similar products or services |
| | **technologies** | technical ways of doing something |

'Competitive' also occurs in these combinations:

| competitive | | |
|---|---|---|
| | **position** | where a company is in relation to its competitors in terms of size, growth, etc. |
| | **pressure** | the force that one competitor can bring to bear in relation to another |
| | **prices** | prices that are similar to or lower than those for similar products |
| | **threat** | something that one competitor may do to weaken another's position |
| | **advantage** **edge** | superior products, performance, etc. that a competitor can offer in relation to others |
| | **strategy** | a plan or plans for success in relation to competitors, and the study of this in business schools |

**17.1** Look at the adjectives describing competition in A opposite. Which is the odd one out, and why?

**17.2** Look at B opposite. Match the two parts of these extracts containing expressions with 'competing'.

1 What is to stop supposedly competing

a bids from mining giants Inco Ltd and Falconbridge Ltd.

2 Commtouch can position itself in the middle of the competing

b suppliers from secretly agreeing to keep prices high?

3 Diamond Fields Resources Inc was the target of competing

c offerings, with prices ranging from $300 to $450.

4 The software is 25 per cent cheaper than competing

d technologies by offering 'unified messaging solutions'.

**17.3** Complete the sentences with words from B opposite that can follow 'competitive'.
1 He was criticized for being too Eurocentric and failing to pay sufficient attention to the competitive .............................. from South east Asia.
2 Businesses can sustain their performances over the long term by having some competitive .............................. to keep them ahead. (2 possibilities)
3 For the money-conscious consumer, alternative retail outlets can offer organic food at more competitive .............................. .
4 First Chicago will enhance its competitive .............................. and boost its financial growth through the transaction, which is expected to add to earnings immediately.
5 Mall stores are under more competitive .............................. than at any time in their 40-year history, with new discounters and superstores increasingly moving in alongside traditional malls.
6 Decades of management theorizing around the world have produced mountains of books, many of which promise to deliver the secrets of success. But there is no consensus on competitive .............................. .

**Over to you**

Think about your organization or one you would like to work for. Who are its fiercest competitors? Why are they a threat?

# 18 Companies and their industries

## Competitive forces

An important strategic thinker is Michael Porter[1]. He defines the five **competitive forces** at work in any industry.

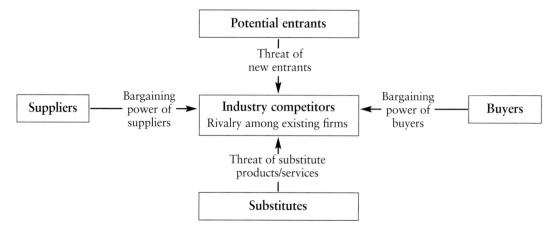

## SWOT analysis

**SWOT** stands for **strengths, weaknesses, opportunities, threats.**

In formulating strategy, a company should look at its strengths and weaknesses in relation to its competitors. For example, a good sales team is a strength and poor internal communication is a weakness.

The company should also look at opportunities and threats in its **environment**: the strength of competitors, government regulation, the way that society is changing etc. These are **external factors**. For example, a change in a country's legislation on broadcasting might present an opportunity for a group that wants to buy a television company there. The change would probably also pose a threat to exisiting broadcasters.

The ways that a company organizes and combines its human resources, know-how, equipment and other assets are what Hamel and Prahalad [2] call its **core competencies**. These are **internal factors**. (See Unit 7)

## Be good at something

Porter says that competitive advantage can be based on:

■ **cost leadership:** offering products or services at the lowest cost; this is one strategy to adopt in **volume industries** where competitors produce large numbers of similar products

■ **differentiation:** offering products or services that give **added value** in terms of quality or service compared to competitors

■ **focus:** using one of the above two strategies to concentrate on a **niche**, a specific part of the market with particular needs.

The danger, says Porter, is when a company does not follow any of these particular strategies and is **stuck in the middle**.

[1] *Competitive Strategy* (Simon & Schuster 1998)
[2] *Competing for the Future* (Harvard Business School Press 1996)

**18.1**

Look at A opposite and the examples (1–5) below of the expressions in the diagram boxes. Match each example to an appropriate form of one of the expressions.

1 Coca-Cola and Pepsi Cola in soft drinks
2 A company that is thinking of selling computer games when it has not sold them before
3 Digital photography in relation to 'traditional' photography
4 Car manufacturers in relation to component manufacturers
5 Component manufacturers in relation to car manufacturers

**18.2** Donna is presenting a SWOT analysis of her travel firm. Complete the table below with the expressions in italics. (The first one has been done for you.)

'We have some very *good locations* for our travel agency shops in cities all over Europe.'

'There may be an *economic slowdown* next year, and *travel* is one of the things people *cut back on* first.'

'We are *big enough to negotiate very good prices* with hotels and airlines.'

'*Internet booking* of travel is *increasing*, and we want to get into this.'

'We need to *improve staff training* – we have a new computer system but a lot of the staff can't get the most from it.'

'There are some very good *online travel companies already established*. They may challenge our position.'

'We have *high staff turnover*.'

'Consumers are looking for *more exotic places* to go on holiday, and *we are planning to offer these destinations*.'

| Strengths | Weaknesses | Opportunities | Threats |
|-----------|------------|---------------|---------|
| Good locations | | | |

**18.3** Look at the mission statements of three companies. Which strategy in C opposite does each correspond to?

1 To make sports cars for discerning enthusiasts with good technical knowledge.
2 To sell clothing more cheaply than the department stores.
3 To sell electrical goods with a high level of after-sales service.

**Over to you**

Analyze your organization or one you would like to work for in relation to the industry it is in, and to the forces in A opposite.

# 19 Key strategic issues

## A Industries and their players

In some industries, like steel or tyres, there are few companies: these industries are **concentrated**. Other industries are **fragmented**: for example there are millions of restaurants worldwide, and even the largest chain, McDonalds, only has a **market share** of less than one per cent in terms of all restaurant meals served worldwide.

Some industries have **low entry barriers** – anyone with a small amount of capital can open a restaurant.

If an industry has low entry barriers and is **attractive** because of its high potential **profitability**, there will always be new **entrants**. This was the case for Internet service providers at the turn of the century with a lot of companies offering this service.

Other industries, like steel, require massive investment in equipment, know-how, etc. – these are **high entry barriers** and new entrants to the industry are rare.

## B Mergers and acquisitions (M&A)

Some companies are very **acquisitive**, buying competitors in their industry or companies in other industries in a series of **acquisitions** or **takeovers**, which it may refer to as **strategic acquisitions**. Or a company may merge or combine as an equal with another company of similar size.

A company may also buy its suppliers and customer companies in a process of **vertical integration**.

The result of this may be an **unwieldy conglomerate**, a holding company with a large number of **subsidiaries**, which may not be easy to manage profitably as a group.

## C Make or buy?

Recent strategic thinking holds that conglomerates are not good. Many conglomerates have **disposed of** or **divested** their **non-core businesses**, selling them off in order to **concentrate on** their **core business**. This is related to the **make or buy decision**, where companies decide whether to produce particular components or perform particular functions **in-house** or to buy them in from an outside supplier. (See Unit 4)

Note: The nouns relating to 'dispose' and 'divest' are '**disposal**' and '**divestment**'. They can be both countable and uncountable nouns. (Compare "divestment" with "investment".)

**19.1**  Complete the crossword with appropriate forms of expressions from A, B and C opposite.

**Across**

7 and 4 Things that make it difficult to get into an industry. (5,8)

9 When a company sells a business activity. (10)

11 See 10 down.

13 If an industry is difficult to get into, entry barriers are .............. . (4)

15 A large group of different businesses. (12)

**Down**

1 A large industry with not many companies is .............. . (12)

2 When two companies join as equal partners, they .............. . (5)

3 A company's most important business activity: its .............. business. (4)

5 A company that buys a lot of other companies is .............. . (11)

6 A large industry with lots of small competitors is .............. . (10)

8 A profitable industry that companies want to get into is .............. . (10)

10 and 11 across When a company buys its suppliers or customers (8, 11)

12 In a fragmented industry, each competitor only has a small market .............. .(5)

14 If an industry is easy to get into, entry barriers are .............. .(3)

**19.2**  An executive in a consumer goods company is talking. Complete what she says with expressions from A and B opposite. (There are two possibilities for one of the gaps.)

'We make a wide range of consumer goods. Over the years we have made a number of (1) .............. .............. , buying companies that fit in with our long-term plan of being the number one consumer goods company in Europe. These (2) .............. mean that we now own a large number of (3) .............. , each with its own brands. We have become an (4) .............. .............. , and all this is very difficult to manage. So we are now reducing the number of brands from 300 to 100, and getting each unit of the company to concentrate on our long-term goal, which is increased (5) .............. and therefore better results for our shareholders. And our increased power will certainly dissuade new (6) .............. from coming into the industry, so our position will be further strengthened.'

Over to you

Think of a recent merger or takeover. What benefits were claimed for it at the time? Have they materialized?

# 20 Innovation

## A  Innovation and the development process

Enrique Sanchez is head of new product development at a large consumer products company:

'We want to **foster creativity** and **innovation** – the development of new ideas. Ours is a large company, but we want to avoid becoming **bureaucratic,** with slow decision making. (See Unit 1)

We encourage **corporate venturing** and **intrapreneurship,** where employees develop **entrepreneurial** activities within the organization, working on their own projects outside the usual frameworks; we allow them to spend 15 per cent of their time on this. We set up **skunk works,** away from the main company sites and outside the usual structures, to work on innovations. This is the way we do our **new product development.** The most famous example of this was IBM, when it developed its PC away from the company's main **research and development** sites.

We firmly believe that companies have only two basic functions: innovation – developing new products and services – and marketing them. Our marketing people are heavily involved in new product development. They get the reactions of **focus groups** – groups of consumers who say what they think of the product – at a very early stage in the **development process.**'

## B  Pioneers and followers

'One problem is to know whether to introduce a product or service before anyone else, or to wait for others to introduce similar products. Some say that if you **bring a product to market** first, you have **first mover advantage** – you can influence the way the market develops. These companies are **trendsetters** or **innovators.** Others say that it's better to be a **follower** and learn from the mistakes of the **pioneers.**'

Note: 'Pioneer' is also a verb.

## C  Shakeout and consolidation

A new or **emerging industry,** perhaps one based on a new **technology,** can be **attractive** – the future **structure** of the industry is not yet **established** and there is room for many competitors. But as growth in the new market slows, smaller competitors with higher costs can no longer compete. They **drop out** or are bought by the larger companies in a process of **shakeout and consolidation,** leaving the larger companies with the resources to **dominate** the industry, which is now **mature.**

**20.1** This article contains words from A opposite. Complete it by choosing the best phrase (a–d) below to go in each of the gaps (1–4).

# INTRAPRENEURSHIP

Increased global competition is forcing large companies to consider more venturesome ways of stimulating product ideas As a theory, intrapreneurship, where large established companies turn to internal 'entrepreneurs' for breakthrough innovations, sounds like a good idea. On the surface, nothing can be more efficient than (1) .............................. .
In practice, things have not been that easy. (2) .............................. many companies which have ventured into the world of intrapreneurship have failed to reap any benefits. After its birth in the 1960s, the concept fell out of favour in the mid-1980s. Fostering different cultures in the same organization has proven to be difficult, while remuneration has also been a problem.
Intrapreneurship seems to have been perceived to be more effort and pain than it was worth. There is an increasing recognition that (3) .............................. Most of the corporate venturing activity in the past has been centred around US companies, and the concept never really caught on in the UK. But increased competition in global markets and the pressure for innovation is forcing Britain's large companies to look for methods to stimulate ideas for new products.
(4) .............................. companies through corporate venturing and intrapreneurship may be given new life in the UK. 'Too many UK companies used to lack global ambition, but now, those who want to compete internationally realize that they need to innovate,' says Jim Martin, director of technology investment at 3i, the venture capital group.

*Financial Times*

a The push for innovation among large

b encouraging innovation among employees so that they come up with mould-breaking products and ensure the company's survival.

c the nature of big companies is to stifle innovation and entrepreneurship, hampering their performance in the global arena.

d Apart from a few examples of success,

**20.2** Complete the sentences with appropriate forms of expressions from B opposite.

1 The alliance put ARM in partnership with Psion, the early .............................. of pocket-sized computers.

2 Freeserve was the first Internet service provider to drop upfront charges and, with this .............................. .............................. .............................. , came to dominate the UK market.

3 But when one company .............................. a successful business, competition inevitably intensifies. Consumers benefit from the resulting cuts in prices and improvements in quality.

4 So far Taiwan has always been a .............................. , making things invented elsewhere more cheaply.

**20.3** Look at the following facts about the development of the market for online book sales. (They are not in chronological order.) Complete the facts with appropriate forms of expressions from C opposite.

1 Some smaller companies stopped selling altogether: they ...

2 There is a trend towards fewer and bigger companies in the market, a trend towards ...

3 Amazon and a few others lead the industry: they ... it.

4 The market is no longer young: it is now ...

Over to you

Is it always difficult for large organizations to come up with innovative ideas and products? How does your organization, or an organization you would like to work for, produce new ideas?

# 21 Preparing for the future

## A Scenario planning

Carmen Ricardo works on long-term strategy in a large oil company:

'My job is to contribute to long-term plans for our future activities. We have to **anticipate** competitors' activities as well as trends in the general **social and economic environment** – we have to be ready to **respond to changes** in society and changes in the economy as a whole. This is called **scenario planning** – we imagine ways in which the energy industry might change and **evolve**, and the place of oil in relation to alternative fuels in 20, 50 or 100 years from now.'

## B Futurology

'I'm a kind of **futurologist** or **futurist**. Of course, **futurology** is not an exact science, and some refer to it as gazing into a **crystal ball**.

But there are ways of predicting the future in a structured manner. There is the **Delphi method**, where a **panel of experts** make their **forecasts** about a subject independently, and the forecasts are circulated to the other members of the group. Each member then comments on the others' observations until all the experts **reach a consensus**: an agreement about what is likely to happen.'

## C Risk management

'A related area is **risk management**. Operating in politically unstable countries is one of the most extreme examples of where we have to manage risk. The dangers there may include **nationalization of assets** by the government.

Elsewhere, we may be accused of working with governments which people do not approve of. We have to think about the impact of this in terms of our reputation for **social responsibility**. (See Unit 41)

There is always the danger of oil spills from ships transporting our oil, with the resulting pollution and associated costs of fines, cleaning up etc. In addition, there is the much greater long-term cost of the negative effect this has on our **image** – the way the company is perceived. A badly-handled oil spill is a **public relations disaster**.

If our computer systems are damaged, for example in a fire, we have **business continuity** plans, involving back-up machines on another site, so that we can carry on working normally.'

These are some of the potential **crises** we face. We try to have **contingency plans** or **crisis management plans** for all the risks we can think of.

**Note:** singular: crisis; plural: crises

**21.1** Carmen Ricardo is talking about the oil industry. Match the underlined words (1–6) to the expressions in A and B opposite that she is referring to.

1 'In studying the trends in the <u>wider picture</u>, we may find that there is increasing consumer demand for alternative fuels such as wind energy, and we have to take account of this change in consumer expectations.'

2 'Of course, <u>we</u> take into account all the factors we can in making our forecasts, but what we do is an inexact science.' (2 possibilities)

3 'One of the problems with <u>this method</u> is that the <u>members</u> will come up with the same ideas as the other experts. There is always a danger when you have <u>an idea that everyone shares</u> that you exclude other possibilities.'

4 'When you make <u>these</u>, you can't avoid looking in the rear view mirror: you tend to base them on what happened in the past.'

5 'Of course, <u>it</u> is an inexact science – the only thing you can say for sure is that the future will be like the past, but different.'

6 'In <u>this area</u>, some of our competitors are talking about scenarios over periods up to 300 years!'

**21.2** Look at C opposite. The questions (1–3) are from shareholders at a tobacco company's annual general meeting. The answers (a–c) are from the company's chief executive. Match the questions to the answers.

1 Are you prepared if the company's executives were kidnapped when working abroad?

2 Do you approve of the government's initiative on preventing children under 16 from smoking?

3 What are you doing to protect the company's image in health issues generally?

a Yes, we are fully aware of our social responsibility in this area.

b Protecting the image of any tobacco company is difficult, but we support, for example, the European Union's plans for stricter health warnings on cigarette packets.
We know our image will suffer if we don't.

c Yes, we have contingency plans to deal with that. A special crisis management team would meet to deal with the situation.

## Over to you

What is the biggest risk for your organization or one you would like to work for?
How has it handled risks in the past? What lessons has it learned?

# 22 The four Ps and the four Cs

## The four Ps

Susanna Chang is marketing manager at the Vermilion mobile phone company:

'Of course, marketing is often defined in terms of:

- **product:** deciding what products and/or services to sell. The word 'product' for us can refer to a product or a service, or a combination of these
- **price:** setting prices that are attractive to customers and that are profitable for the company
- **place:** finding suitable **distribution channels** and **outlets** to reach these customer groups
- **promotion:** all the activities, not just advertising, used to support the product – everything from pre-sales information to after-sales service.

These are the **four Ps** of the **marketing mix**, the factors that we use in different combinations for different products and different potential buyers.

So my job is much more than organizing advertising campaigns. I work with engineers, finance people and other senior managers to find **offerings** – products, services and combinations of these – that will appeal to customers.'

## B The four Cs

'But I find it helps us more to look at the marketing effort from the point of view of customers, rather than the company, when we consider the **four Cs**:

- **customer solution:** we aim to find a solution to a customer 'problem' by offering the right combination of products and services to satisfy particular customer needs. Pay-as-you-go was a dream solution for parents worried about children running up big phone bills
- **customer cost:** the price paid by the customer for the product. It includes the 'price' related to not buying another product of the same or another type. For example, someone who buys a sophisticated mobile may not then have the money to buy a laptop computer that they wanted
- **convenience:** distributing our products in the way that is most convenient for each type of customer. We have to decide, for instance, how many new shops to open and where they should be
- **communication** with the customer: customers are informed about products through advertising and so on, but the communication is two-way because customers also communicate with us, for example through telephone helplines. This is a good way for us to find out more about what our customers want, and to change or improve our offering, and to get ideas for new offerings.

Thinking of the marketing mix in these terms helps us maintain a true **customer orientation** or **customer focus**.'

**22.1** Susanna Chang continues to talk about her organization. Find which 'P' of the marketing mix in A opposite she is referring to in each of her statements.

1 We want to offer calls at a lower cost than our competitors.

2 We don't put our own brand on mobile phones, but we sell phones for use on different call plans: both pre-paid and monthly-billed customers.

3 We advertise heavily on television and in the national press.

4 We have our own high-street outlets, and we also sell through the big electrical goods stores.

5 We phone existing customers to try to persuade them to buy more sophisticated phones which have a higher profit margin.

6 We sponsor classical music concerts.

**22.2** A mobile phone customer is talking about a recent mobile phone purchase. Find which 'C' in B opposite he is referring to in each of his statements.

1 I was looking for a phone that gives me Internet access.

2 I wanted the phone to be delivered to my door.

3 I had some questions about how to use the phone, so I phoned the customer helpline. They were very helpful.

4 My budget's limited – I had the money to buy a phone or a computer, but not both.

5 I love the modern design of the phone. I was looking for something that looks fashionable and up-to-date.

6 I like the TV advertisements – I only noticed them after I bought the phone, but they persuaded me that I'd made the right choice.

**22.3** Look at the expressions in A and B opposite and say if these statements are true or false.

1 Another word for a shop is a 'let-out'.
2 Distribution channels are used to get goods from producers to consumers.
3 A product or service, or a combination of these sold together, is an offering.
4 The four Ps are also referred to as the marketing mixture.
5 Sellers with a customer focus are only concerned with the technical excellence of their products as an end in itself.

Over to you

Think of something that you bought recently. Describe your purchase in terms of the four Cs.
Then describe it from the seller's point of view in terms of the four Ps.

# 23 Customer satisfaction

## A The customer

From the point of view of sellers …

| | | is when customers … |
|---|---|---|
| customer | satisfaction | are happy with your products |
| | delight | are extremely happy with your products |
| | allegiance loyalty | continue to buy from you |
| | dissatisfaction | are not happy with your products |
| | defection | stop buying your products |

## B Customer delight

When you get what you hoped for as a customer, your **expectations** are **met** and there is **customer satisfaction**. Products, sadly, often **fall below** expectations.

When expectations are **exceeded**, there may even be delight, extreme satisfaction, but this partly depends on how **involved** you are in the purchase. There is a difference in your degree of **involvement** when you buy different products. For example, there is low involvement when you buy something ordinary like petrol, and high involvement when you purchase something emotionally important such as a family holiday.

## C Customer dissatisfaction

Research shows that 95 per cent of dissatisfied customers don't complain, but just change suppliers. Satisfied customers create new business by telling up to 12 other people. Dissatisfied ones will tell up to 20 people[1]. **Word-of-mouth** is a powerful form of advertising.

Some say that encouraging **customer loyalty** is important for profitability. They say that **customer retention**, keeping existing customers, is key. Getting **repeat business** is five times cheaper than finding new customers. (For another view, see the article opposite.)

**Customer defection** must be reduced as much as possible of course, but a company can learn from its mistakes by asking those who do leave why they defected; this is **lost customer analysi**s.

Services like mobile phone and cable TV companies have to reduce **churn,** the percentage of customers who change suppliers or who stop using the service altogether each year. This is very costly – the companies would prefer, of course, to keep existing customers and add more in order to build their **customer base**.

[1] Philip Kotler: *Marketing Management* (Prentice Hall 2000, Chapter 2)

**23.1** Match the two parts of these sentences containing expressions from A opposite.

1 There is overwhelming evidence that customer satisfaction is correlated
2 With our customer loyalty scheme,
3 The financial services industry is struggling, partly because
4 The Internet service provider has introduced flat-rate
5 Excellent product quality has helped them to build strong customer allegiance and
6 Customer delight is more

a any existing borrower who moves home and continues to borrow with us is entitled to a one per cent discount.
b with employee satisfaction.
c prices in an attempt to stop customer defections.
d of customer dissatisfaction with high charges.
e than just mere satisfaction.
f increasing market share.

**23.2**

## Dispensing with loyalty

The assumption that loyal customers are more profitable is debatable – companies need to focus on mutual benefit. Will we ever really get to grips with the concept of loyalty, or would it be better to dispense with it altogether? (1) ................................... It costs less money to serve loyal customers. They provide the best opportunities to sell more. But as companies experiment with loyalty marketing, doubts are coming to the surface. (2) ................................... In most categories, the big spenders tend also to be buyers of different products. It's the small spenders who buy the same brand again and again, but only very infrequently. This 100% loyal customer is worth hardly anything compared to the promiscuous 'flitter'. Conclusion: the 80/20 rule rules. (3) ................................... Ehrenburg's scepticism was matched by experienced business-to-business marketers who quickly pointed out that the most financially significant 'loyal' accounts are often the least profitable. (4) ...................................

*Brand Strategy*

This article contains words from B and C opposite. Complete it by choosing the best sentence (a–d) to go in each of the gaps (1–4).

a Don't go for loyalty per se, go for the 20% of customers who really count, no matter how 'loyal' they might be.
b One of the earliest doubters was Professor Andrew Ehrenburg of South Bank University, whose long experience with purchasing data led him to argue that often the most 'loyal' customers are the least profitable.
c The big idea behind loyalty is that loyal customers are more profitable. Keeping existing customers is cheaper than finding new ones.
d They're the product of big, powerful customers getting such good deals that there's hardly any margin left for the seller.

Now say which of these sentences better sums up the article.

1 Loyal customers are not necessarily the most profitable.
2 Customers who spend the most are the most loyal.

**Over to you**

Look again at the article above. Which view of customer loyalty does your organization, or one you would like to work for, take?

# 24 Knowing your customers 1

## A Data and databases

'Hi, I'm John. I'm head of **data management** at a big supermarket chain. Customers can get money back by using our **loyalty card** when they go shopping. Loyalty cards allow customers to collect points that can be **redeemed against** future purchases, either with us, or with other retailers in the same scheme. This gives us masses of data about our customers, which we then hold on our **database**. We can follow what each of our customers buys, and **enrich the database** with this information.'

## B Data mining

'Of course, with all the information we have on our computers in our **data warehouses**, powerful computers are needed to analyze it. This analysis is called **data mining**. We look for particular patterns in **consumer behaviour**. The data can be used to **target** particular types of customer. We build **consumer profiles**. For example, if someone has bought wine in the past, special offers are sent to them so they get reduced prices on future purchases of wine.

There are issues of **privacy** and **confidentiality** that we have to be careful about – customers have the right to check the information that we hold about them. We must be careful to obey the law on **data protection**.' (See Unit 29)

> BrE behaviour;
> AmE behavior

| | |
|---|---|
| LEMONADE | €1.1 |
| * STILL WATER | €0.90 |
| * WINE (RED) | €6.80 |
| * JUICE (ORANGE) | €1.25 |
| ICE (APPLE) | €? |

## C Customer relationship management

'All this is part of the wider picture of **customer relationship management (CRM)** – getting to know your customers. Dealing with them as individuals is our ultimate goal, but we are still a long way from this ideal of **one-to-one marketing**.

This has also been described as **segment-of-one marketing**. The computer maker Dell may be on its way to this ideal – it puts together its products according to the specifications of individual customers in a process of **mass customization**.'

**24.1** Read the article relating to the ideas in A and B opposite. Then complete the sentences below with expressions from the article.

---

### Intelligent tills that check you out along with your goods are now part of our daily life

Have you ever wondered what the real motive is behind supermarket loyalty cards? They are a front for tying you up with the things that you buy. Till records are no longer lists of anonymous purchases, but preferences attached to real, reachable people.

One day you will turn on your Internet terminal, log on to your customary grocery supplier and will be greeted with a personalised message such as: 'Special offer on Chateauneuf du Pape.' The system will have noted your love of red wine at around £7 a bottle and will try to increase your spending on it. When you have negotiated this temptation, you will check your regular list and make some changes as Auntie, who is staying for the weekend, likes that revolting tinned salmon and, as the cat has just been run over, you cancel its food. Otherwise, it's the order as usual.

So entertainment sellers will log what we watch and when: football on Monday, cartoons with the kids on Tuesday, documentaries on Wednesday, and so on. You will be reminded of the special two-hour episode of your favourite soap opera to be released at midnight at a special price.

This model of a supply being influenced by our own behaviour is already part of some email systems. If you regularly answer emails from Jack before anybody else, the system can put Jack at the top of your list every morning. But if a deal falls through with Jack, he will slip down the running order. Soon the same kind of system will help to regulate our viewing behaviour. In a world of multi-channel, pay-per-view, unscheduled television, every minute you mess about with your remote control is a minute of unsold entertainment.

*The Guardian*

---

1 Retailers learn about customers' buying habits by looking at ............................ ................................ , the information stored on computer as customers check out with their purchases.
2 These can be matched to specific individuals: they are not ............................... .
3 The amount you pay for a particular type of goods is your ............................... on those goods.
4 Retailers and entertainment sellers watch and record, or ............................... , the behaviour of customers and viewers.
5 If a product or programme becomes available at a particular time, it is ............................... at that time.
6 When something is influenced by what an individual does, it changes according to their ............................... .

**24.2** Match the two parts of these extracts containing expressions from opposite C.

1 Citizens' rights organizations are becoming more and more concerned

2 One expert has defined customer relationship management as

3 We need to create one-to-one marketing and build

4 Under the Data Protection Act, people have the right

a 'identifying, attracting and retaining the most valuable customers to sustain profitable growth'.

b one-to-one relationships. We have to offer our customers sets of services tailored to their needs.

c to ask to see the information that companies and government departments hold about them.

d about the problems of privacy and confidentiality on marketing databases.

---

### Over to you

Think about your organization or one you would like to work for. What kind of information does it hold about its customers?

As a customer, what kind of information do you think it is acceptable for organizations to hold about you?

# 25

# Knowing your customers 2

## A Segmentation

A **segment** is a group of customers or potential customers with similar characteristics, needs and requirements. **Segmentation**, which can be done in various ways, allows marketers to identify and **differentiate** between the needs of the **target groups** of customers that make up a particular market. They may offer different products to different segments, or the same product, marketing it in different ways. For example, power tools are designed and marketed differently for professional users and do-it-yourself enthusiasts.

Note: 'Segment' is also used as a verb.

## B Customer groups: demographic and behavioural segmentation

In **demographic segmentation** customers are divided up on the basis of **occupation** and **social class**: middle class, working class, etc. In the UK, marketers classify customers demographically as:

A    professionals such as senior business executives and senior civil servants
B    people with very responsible jobs such as middle managers, heads of local government departments, and so on
C1   all others doing non-manual jobs: technicians, nurses, etc.
C2   skilled manual workers
D    semi-skilled and unskilled manual workers
E    those on the lowest income levels, such as pensioners.

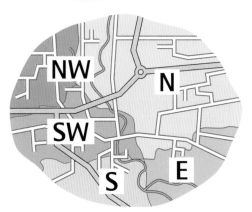

In Britain, marketers also use a system called **ACORN**, which is **a classification of residential neighbourhoods**, a system that assumes that people from a particular area will have a similar social background. It can be used to predict likely purchases of everything from cat food to financial products.

Customers can also be divided up by **behavioural segmentation**: why, when and how often they buy a particular product, their attitude towards it, etc. Identifying people who eat popcorn at the cinema is an example of behavioural segmentation based on **situation of use**.

## C Customer groups: lifestyle and psychographic segmentation

People from a particular social class may spend their money in particular ways, but it can be more useful to look at people's **lifestyles**, the overall pattern of how they live, what they buy etc. Here, **values**, **opinions**, **activities** and **interests** are important.

**Psychographics** is the activity of attempting to categorize people in this way. For example, the VALS system[1] divides people into groups such as *Fulfilleds*: mature people who like solid products that give value for money, and *Experiencers*: young, impulsive people who spend a lot on clothes, music, etc.

This information is often collected by means of **questionnaires** used to **profile** different kinds of buyers.

[1] You can do the VALS questionnaire and get your own VALS profile at the SRI Consulting Business Intelligence site: www.sric-bi.com

**25.1**  Complete the statements by people working for different organizations with appropriate forms of expressions from A and B opposite. (Some expressions are used more than once.)

1 'I work for a food products company. We make a powder that can be added to hot milk to make a nutritious drink. It is used to make two different products and is sold under two different names, to mothers who feed it to their babies, and to old people who drink it to get important vitamins. This is the basis of our ............................... . Of course, these are two entirely different ............................... .'

2 'I market beer. With our Heavyside Brew, we go for heavy drinkers of beer who drink it in pubs, never at home: this is our ............................... ............................... for this product.

3 'We sell car insurance. We calculate the premiums using ............................... because this tells us about the areas our customers live in and their ............................... ............................... : we are great believers in ............................... ............................... .'

4 'I work for a political party. When we knock on people's doors and ask them to vote for us, we never try to persuade people who are hostile to us. We concentrate on people whose attitudes are favourable to us in some way, even if they haven't voted for us before, and this ............................... ............................... allows us to target our resources better.'

5 'I work on health campaigns to discourage people from smoking. One of the most important ............................... ............................... is young people from 12 to 18. We want to discourage them from taking up smoking in the first place.'

**25.2**  Look at C opposite and match the two parts of these descriptions of VALS types. (The first one has been done for you.)

1 Experiencers are young, enthusiastic people who spend a lot on clothes,  
2 Strugglers are poorer, elderly people who are loyal  
3 Actualizers are successful, active people with  
4 Believers are conservative traditionalists who prefer familiar  
5 Makers are practical family-oriented people who buy practical,  
6 Strivers are insecure people without much money but who buy stylish  

a to familiar brands.  
b cultivated, expensive tastes.  
c for example, without planning for a long time what they are going to buy.  
d functional products such as tools.  
e products to imitate those with more money.  
f products and established brands.  

**Over to you**

Which demographic segment in B opposite do you belong to?

Think of a product you have bought recently and analyze your purchase in terms of behavioural segmentation.

# 26 Brands and branding

## A Brand equity

A **brand** is a name given to a product or group of products so that it can be easily recognized. 'The most distinctive power of professional marketers is their ability to **create, maintain, protect** and **enhance** (strengthen the power of) **brands**,' says Philip Kotler[1]. This is reflected in the value that companies put on their brands. For example, BMW paid $60 million for the Rolls Royce name alone, not including any material assets such as manufacturing plant.

'Brand' often occurs in these combinations:

| | | |
|---|---|---|
| brand | awareness<br>familiarity<br>recognition | the degree to which people know a brand |
| | promise | what people expect from a brand |
| | preference | when consumers like one brand more than another |
| | image | all the ways that people think about a brand |
| | equity | the value of a brand to its owners, as sometimes shown on a firm's balance sheet |

These combinations are some of the issues in **branding**, the art and science of using brands.

## B Brand positioning and differentiation

A firm can **position** a **brand** by emphasizing its characteristics and benefits in relation to other brands – this is **brand positioning**, which can be represented on a **positioning map**.

Here is an example of a positioning map for different brands of breakfast food.

**Differentiation** is when a company designs a product in a way that distinguishes it from competitors' brands and communicates the comparative benefits to customers in its sales documentation, advertising etc. For example, a UK mobile phone company ran a campaign addressed to the 'hard-nosed businessman'. This was an effort to differentiate its:

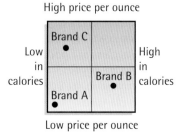

- business services from those for private users
- business services from the less-targeted services offered by other mobile phone companies.

## C Brand stretching

A **flagship brand** is the most important one owned by an organization – for example 'Coke' is the most famous of the many soft drinks brands owned by Coca-Cola. A **generic brand** is one used on a variety of different products. For example, the brand name 'Nestlé' is used on all the food products the company owns, even if another brand name is also used on some of the products.

**Brand stretching** or **brand extension** is when a company uses an existing brand name for new types of product. Some marketers say that there are limits to this. They say that brand stretching can lead to **brand dilution**, making the brand less powerful.

[1] *Marketing Management* (Prentice Hall 2000, p.415)

**26.1** Complete the article with expressions from A and B opposite, choosing the correct alternative.

> ## Death of the salesmen: The end of door to door selling leaves financial brands with an identity crisis
>
> As the men from the Pru, Britannic Assurance and Sun Life of Canada hang up their hats and make their last house calls, companies with financial (1) brands/branding/brand positioning built on friendly face-to-face contact are re-evaluating the way they market their brands. The death of the life assurance salesmen mirrors a move across the financial industry to shun direct customer contact in favour of "remote" communication via the telephone and the Internet.
>
> But both the Britannic and Prudential brands are based on face-to-face advice. Now the companies must maintain the personable feel of their brands, and consumers" trust. "The entire (2)preference/awareness/positioning of these companies is built on a face-to-face service: it's their brand (3) promise/familiarity/preference. When you take the personal touch away, that promise is broken. It risks damaging the brand (4) awareness/equity/recognition,"
>
> says David Gray, director of Creative Leap, the branding agency for Marks & Spencer's financial services.
> "The direct sales force and branch staff have been the face of the brand. But the accountants have made the decisions from the cost-cutting point of view, not the (5) branding/promise/awareness one. It leaves them with questions about who they are and what they stand for. Consumers are already disappointed with financial services: this is just another nail in the coffin," says Gray.
>
> *The Guardian*

**26.2** Complete the statements with appropriate forms of words from the article above.

1 Two types of communication are mentioned: ............................-............................-............................ and ............................ . The first type of communication refers to salesmen making ............................ ............................ . This human interaction gave the brands of financial services companies a ............................ feel.

2 When customers rely on a brand, they have a sense of ............................ in the brand. This feeling was broken when salesmen no longer visited customers and the personal ............................ was taken away. This also led to the feeling that the brand ............................ had been broken.

3 If financial services companies are not careful, their brands risk being ............................ by the move to telephone and Internet selling. Customers already feel that their expectations of financial services companies have not been met: they are already ............................ .

**26.3** Look at the article again and answer the questions.

1 Find an example of a) face-to-face contact and b) remote contact.
2 What two things happen when a company changes the way it deals with customers, for example by taking away the 'personal touch'?
3 Find idiomatic expressions that mean:
   a 'finish their work'.   b 'follows a similar trend'.   c 'a further negative factor'.

**26.4** Look at B and C opposite. What are these situations examples of?

1 A marketer of cat food called Miaow attempts to persuade cat owners that the product is nutritious, tastes good and makes cats' fur healthy and shiny.
2 The marketer of Miaow starts to use the same name for dog food. (2 expressions)
3 Consumers complain that Miaow is a more suitable name for cat food and that they now have less faith in both the cat food and the dog food.

## Over to you

Think about your organization or one you would like to work for. What are its brands?

# 27 Global brands

## A Steps abroad 1

Gianna Paolozzi is marketing manager for GI, an Italian company that makes ice cream:

'We started to get orders from Scandinavia and we wondered how people had heard about us! So we contacted **agents** there who could help us to sell the ice cream – this was **indirect export**, and they represented us. These **exclusive agents** each had their own **sales area**.

Sales grew, and we moved on to **direct export**: we no longer used agents but handled exports ourselves. We had an **export manager** based here in Italy, but she spent 11 months a year travelling in our different markets.'

## B Steps abroad 2

'Then we started **licensing** our production techniques to companies abroad, selling them the **rights** to produce ice cream **under licence** for their markets. In Thailand, for example, we had a **licensing agreement** with a company to produce and market our ice cream there. But in China, we signed a **joint venture** agreement with an established food processing company who knew the market well – we treated them as equal partners. The agreement worked very well for five years but then we decided to make a **direct investment** in China, building ice cream production plants and marketing our products ourselves.'

> BrE: 'licence' – noun, 'license' – verb;
> AmE: 'license' – noun and verb

## C Think global, act local

The world as one market?

'Some companies offer exactly the same products all over the world. Theirs are **global offerings**. But we try to **adapt** our products to individual markets and local tastes. For example, some countries prefer sweeter flavours in ice cream. Marketers talk, informally, about **glocalization**.

GI is now a **global brand** – our products are enjoyed in 120 countries all over the world.'

**27.1** Complete the emails from a Canadian company called AFM (Advanced Farm Machinery) with correct forms of expressions from A and B opposite. (Some expressions are used more than once.)

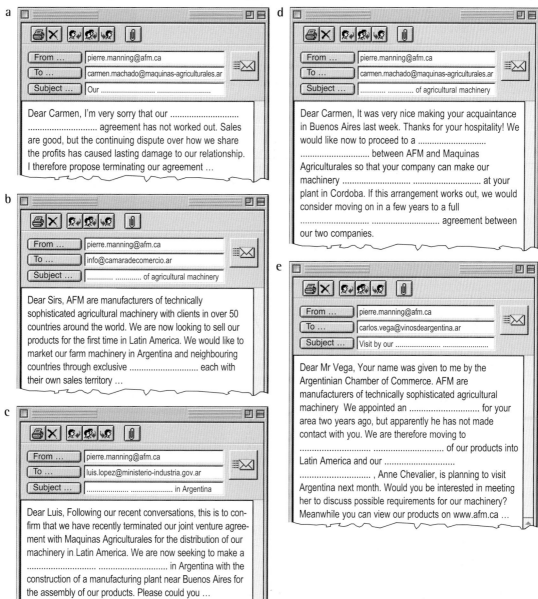

**a**

From … pierre.manning@afm.ca
To … carmen.machado@maquinas-agriculturales.ar
Subject … Our ..............................................

Dear Carmen, I'm very sorry that our ...............................
............................. agreement has not worked out. Sales are good, but the continuing dispute over how we share the profits has caused lasting damage to our relationship. I therefore propose terminating our agreement …

**b**

From … pierre.manning@afm.ca
To … info@camaradecomercio.ar
Subject … ............. ............. of agricultural machinery

Dear Sirs, AFM are manufacturers of technically sophisticated agricultural machinery with clients in over 50 countries around the world. We are now looking to sell our products for the first time in Latin America. We would like to market our farm machinery in Argentina and neighbouring countries through exclusive ............................. each with their own sales territory …

**c**

From … pierre.manning@afm.ca
To … luis.lopez@ministerio-industria.gov.ar
Subject … .................... .................... in Argentina

Dear Luis, Following our recent conversations, this is to con-firm that we have recently terminated our joint venture agree-ment with Maquinas Agriculturales for the distribution of our machinery in Latin America. We are now seeking to make a ............................. ............................. in Argentina with the construction of a manufacturing plant near Buenos Aires for the assembly of our products. Please could you …

**d**

From … pierre.manning@afm.ca
To … carmen.machado@maquinas-agriculturales.ar
Subject … ............. ............. of agricultural machinery

Dear Carmen, It was very nice making your acquaintance in Buenos Aires last week. Thanks for your hospitality! We would like now to proceed to a .............................
............................. between AFM and Maquinas Agriculturales so that your company can make our machinery ............................. ............................. at your plant in Cordoba. If this arrangement works out, we would consider moving on in a few years to a full ............................. ............................. agreement between our two companies.

**e**

From … pierre.manning@afm.ca
To … carlos.vega@vinosdeargentina.ar
Subject … Visit by our .............................

Dear Mr Vega, Your name was given to me by the Argentinian Chamber of Commerce. AFM are manufacturers of technically sophisticated agricultural machinery We appointed an ............................. for your area two years ago, but apparently he has not made contact with you. We are therefore moving to ............................. ............................. of our products into Latin America and our .............................
............................. , Anne Chevalier, is planning to visit Argentina next month. Would you be interested in meeting her to discuss possible requirements for our machinery? Meanwhile you can view our products on www.afm.ca …

Now put the emails into their probable chronological order.

**27.2** Look at section C. Does each of the companies 1–3 below a) have a standard global offering, or b) adapt its products to specific markets?

1 a washing machine company that makes top-loading machines for some markets where kitchens are small
2 a furniture company that sells exactly the same products round the world
3 an accountancy firm that prepares accounts in different ways in different countries so that they conform with local accountancy rules

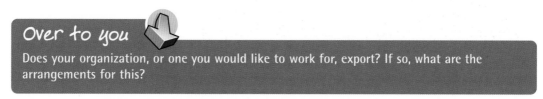

**Over to you**

Does your organization, or one you would like to work for, export? If so, what are the arrangements for this?

# 28 The IT revolution

## A Broadband Internet

One of the key issues in **information technology (IT)** is, of course, the future of the Internet.

The Internet may not have 'changed everything' in the economy, as some predicted a few years ago, but it is still growing fast. On **landlines** – fixed telephone lines – high-speed **broadband access** is making it faster and easier to use the Internet and to **download files** with text, pictures, video, etc.

Faster connections also allow better use of some **applications** such as **video-conferencing**, where people in two or more locations can see and talk to each other.

Note: Broadband is also known as DSL (direct subscriber link) in the USA.

## B Mobile Internet

The next step is accessing the Internet via **mobile devices** such as mobile phones and **PDAs (personal digital assistants**, also referred to as **handhelds**).

High-speed access is already available on **wireless LAN (local area network**) systems, also known as **wi-fi**. To access the Internet in this way, you have to be in a particular **hotspot**: a place such as a café or airport terminal, which is equipped with the network.

High speeds are promised for **3G** or **third generation systems** offered by mobile phone companies, who paid very high prices for the licences to operate them. They were expecting high demand by mobile phone users for a wide range of information and entertainment services, for example replays of football highlights. Time will tell if these prices were justified.

## C Moore's Law

Another factor in these developments is **Moore's Law**, the principle that the **computing power** of a particular size of **computer chip**, the basic component of computers, will roughly double every 18 months. This law can also be used to talk about cost – the cost of a particular unit of computing power will continue to halve every 18 months for the foreseeable future. The law is named after Gordon Moore, co-founder of the chip company Intel, who made the prediction in 1965.

**28.1** Complete the crossword with expressions from A, B and C opposite.

**Across**

3 See 12 down.

8 Demand for these services is as yet uncertain. (5,10)

9 You can find these in some public places. (5,4,8)

11 Non-mobile phone lines. (9)

14 What Moore's Law relates to. (9,5)

15 You can do this much faster with broadband. (8,5)

17 and 13 down Things like mobile phones and PDAs. (6,7)

**Down**

1 This device is for individual users: it's ............... . (7)

2 When people in different places use the Internet to see and hear each other, they are video-............... . (12)

4 No cables attached. (8)

5 A computer's basic component. (4)

6 Another name for PDAs. (9)

7 A place offering wi-fi for Internet access. (7)

10 Broadband gives high-speed ............... . (6)

12 and 3 across A principle relating to the cost of computing power. (6,3)

13 See 17 across.

16 Another name for wireless LANs. (2–2)

**28.2** Use Moore's Law in C opposite to do the following calculation: in 1974, the cost of a particular size of computer memory chip was $10,000. By 1997, the cost for the same unit had fallen to:

a  $1,000          b  $100          c  $1

Gordon Moore

*Over to you*

Do you think mobile devices are suitable for accessing the Internet? Think of the websites you visit when using a PC: are they suitable for viewing on a smaller device? What sort of services would you like to access – replays of football matches, online shopping, weather forecasts ... ?

# 29 Internet security

## A Attack and defence

Melissa Vorster is a consultant on Internet security:

'I work with companies to try to prevent **hackers** from penetrating their computer systems in order to steal or destroy the information on them. Hackers are people who may write programs designed to **overload** an organization's system with requests for information so that users cannot access it. We call this a **denial of service attack**, and it causes huge inconvenience for customers and lost business for companies.

Another problem is **viruses**. A virus is a small program designed to make computers misfunction, despite the **firewalls** and **anti-virus programs** that we **install** as the technical defences against them.'

## B Cybercrime

'Some companies that I work with sell goods and services over the Internet and need to reassure their customers that their credit card details are safe and will not be stolen by hackers. Credit card details and other confidential information to be transmitted is **encrypted**, or coded, so that it cannot be read by others. Companies that sell on the Internet will display the level of **encryption** that users of their site benefit from.

This is a defence against one form of **cybercrime** – criminal activity on the Internet.'

## C Privacy and confidentiality

'When someone uses the Internet, they leave an **electronic trail**, a record of the sites they visit, and if they buy something, their personal details. This raises issues of **privacy** and **confidentiality**. Who should have the right to access and analyze this information?

This is all part of the debate about the powers of **surveillance** (the powers to watch and examine the activities of private individuals) that **law enforcement agencies,** such as the police, should have. Critics call this **snooping**, and there are big issues of **human rights law** and **civil liberties** at stake because these are freedoms that ordinary people should be able to enjoy.'

**29.1** Replace the underlined phrases in the headlines with expressions from A and B opposite.

1
**Badly-intentioned intruders** penetrate Pentagon computers

2
Xenon's system down for 5 hours in **action designed to exclude access**

3
Companies' system defences withstand latest attack    (2 possibilities)

4
Latest methods of **translating to 'code'** make confidential messages unreadable by outsiders

5
**Illegal internet activity** increases three-fold

6
**Programs designed to slow computer functions** found in attachments to company emails

**29.2** Complete the article with expressions from C opposite. (Two expressions are used twice.)

# Snooping system is illegal, say police

(1) ............................. powers allowing law enforcement agencies to access the communications records of telephone and Internet users are in such a legal mess that they are untenable, one of Britain's most senior police officers will today tell a parliamentary inquiry. Jim Gamble, assistant chief constable of the national crime squad and head of the association of chief police officers' data communications group, will admit to MPs that the current system to access web, email and phone logs is illegal under (2) .............................. ............................. , the Guardian has learned.

He will also complain that legal difficulties with the legislation passed to resolve this problem are "leaving the communications industry uncertain of the legal position". His astonishing intervention on behalf of the UK law enforcement community piles pressure on ministers to rethink their raft of (3) ............................. measures. These will require communications providers to stockpile customers' records for long periods and allow (4) ............................. ............................. ............................. to access them without need for a judicial or executive warrant.

Richard Allan, Liberal Democrat home affairs spokesman and the inquiry's joint chair, said: "Jim Gamble's submission reflects a climate change in the Home Office and the police. They have now realised that this is a matter of major public interest and are trying to strike a better balance between catching criminals and protecting the (5) ............................. of innocent citizens."

At the moment, companies store data only for as long as necessary for their own purposes, such as billing and marketing. (6) ............................. ............................. ............................. are able to access an individual's records only if they can convince the service provider that they should be exempt from data protection laws because there is enough evidence to believe the person is involved in wrongdoing.

*The Guardian*

**29.3** Find words or phrases in the article above that mean:

1 not able to be legally enforced
2 series of actions
3 keep large numbers of
4 formal statement
5 change in attitude
6 take a fairer approach to
7 not included in

## Over to you

Consider these ways of communicating confidential information, such as credit card details, to a company:

• speaking on the phone.    • sending a fax.    • completing a form on the Internet.

• posting a written form.    • sending an email.

Which do you feel is most secure, and which least? Why?

# 30 E-commerce: after boom and bust

## A Old economy, new economy

In the late 1990s companies raised vast amounts of money from investors for **e-commerce** Internet sites, both **business-to-consumer** (B2C) and **business-to-business** (B2B). B2B, where businesses obtain supplies using the Internet, is also referred to as **e-procurement**.

Commentators talked about the **old economy**, with companies doing business in traditional ways, and the **new economy**, with companies doing business over the Internet. This was the **dotcom frenzy**, the period of large numbers of **Internet start-ups**, many promising riches for investors, some of whom believed that the usual laws of economics no longer applied. However, most of the sites from that time have now disappeared.

## B B2C

In business-to-consumer e-commerce, sites were set up selling everything from pet food to clothes. Among the survivors, there are companies like Amazon, **pure-play** (exclusively) **online sellers**, with no traditional shops – no **bricks-and-mortar outlets**. This is **pure e-tailing**.

Other retail organizations are **clicks-and-mortar** ones, combining e-commerce with sales through traditional outlets. Some old-economy companies, like the UK supermarket group Tesco, use e-commerce in conjunction with its existing operations – it did not have to invest in a whole new expensive **infrastructure** of new computer systems, warehouses, etc. to take care of its **e-fulfilment**, processing and delivering orders.

> BrE: e-fulfilment;
> AmE: e-fulfillment

## C B2B

In business-to-business e-commerce, groups of companies can set up **public exchanges**. For example, the WorldWide Retail Exchange allows companies to bid to supply participating retailers in a **reverse auction** on the Internet – the supplier offering the lowest price gets the contract.

There are also **private exchanges**, where a single company deals with suppliers in this way. Some companies prefer to use this form of e-commerce because they do not want to indicate their requirements to their competitors, thus revealing their current activities.

Both public and private exchanges are also referred to as **e-marketplaces**, **trading hubs** or **trading platforms**.

**30.1** Match the two parts of these sentences containing expressions from A opposite.

1 B2B e-commerce can cut firms' costs because

2 The company operates four e-commerce sites,

3 There was a huge temptation for me to follow the dotcom frenzy

4 Management theorists agreed that old-fashioned command-and-control management styles would not work

5 There has been a trend for investors to shift funds out of the technology, media and telecoms sectors

6 As the early web firms were addressing the business-to-consumer market,

a the low prices they promised consumers meant that the scale of their business had to be enormous.

b but I felt more comfortable investing in a fund whose core holdings are large multinationals.

c it reduces procurement costs, both by making it easier to find the cheapest supplier and through efficiency gains.

d selling books, CDs, DVDs and computer games.

e in the new economy, where creativity and innovation are everything.

f back into old economy companies such as oil and car producers.

**30.2** Complete the sentences with appropriate forms of expressions from B and C opposite.

1 Retailer A sells clothes in shops and also over the Internet: it has ...............................-...............................-............................... outlets.

2 Retailer B sells books and CDs on the Internet and has no shops: it has no ...............................-...............................-............................... ..............................., so it's involved in ............................... ...............................-............................... .

3 Retailer B has built massive warehouses and developed sophisticated computer systems: it has invested in the ............................... necessary for ...............................-............................... .

4 Household goods manufacturer C has set up a ............................... ............................... where it asks for bids from suppliers.

5 Defence companies D, E, F and G have got together to form a ............................... ............................... in order to get competitive bids from a range of suppliers.

6 Suppliers to D, E, F and G submit prices for particular projects in a ............................... ..............................., and the supplier offering the lowest price wins the contract.

7 Manufacturer C and Companies D, E, F and G run different kinds of ............................... (-)............................... . (three possible expressions)

Over to you

Have you ever bought something over the Internet? If so, what was your experience of the website, delivery of goods, time taken etc.

# 31 Knowledge management

## A Sharing knowledge

Leila Vidal is **chief knowledge officer** at a multinational insurance company:

'Everything we do is based on **knowledge** – knowledge of our customers and what they need to insure against, knowledge of our competitors, and so on.

We want to make sure that this knowledge is shared by everyone in the organization. For example, subsidiaries in different countries can benefit from the **competencies** and **know-how** (theoretical and practical knowledge) in other parts of the company so they

- don't have to **reinvent the wheel** and develop something that has already been done elsewhere;
- can raise their standards of efficiency to reach the **best practices** in the organization (see Unit 15).

This is all part of **knowledge sharing**.'

reinventing the wheel

## B The learning organization

'One way of making knowledge available to everyone is through the **company intranet**: information is made available on the company's computer system so that all employees have access to it. For example, in project development, they can look at how past projects were organized, how much they cost, etc. They can see new ideas that were proposed but that were never taken up. Employees can **tap into** a vast amount of information.

Knowledge is our **intellectual capital** and we want to exploit it and develop it. We are great believers in **professional development** – employees spend 10 per cent of their time on training courses. (See Unit 4) We think of ourselves as a **learning organization** and we centralize our training at our own **company university**, using our own managers as trainers, as well as bringing trainers in from outside.

We have to fight against managers who think that they can enhance their power by **hogging knowledge**, i.e. keeping it for themselves. They argue, wrongly, that employees should be informed on a **need-to-know basis**.

Another problem is managing this knowledge and making it available in usable ways, so that people aren't overwhelmed by **information overload**.'

**31.1** Read the article relating to the ideas in A and B opposite. Then complete the sentences below with appropriate forms of expressions from the article.

# The next big thing

Is Knowledge Management an electronic or a people revolution? asks Adrian Barrett

Whilst knowledge management is a concept that has its roots in the libraries of antiquity, its metamorphosis into today's hot management topic has been based on recent developments in technology which have allowed the effective management of huge amounts of information.

Many international organisations now use intranets to make the sharing of information possible across offices separated by thousands of miles and disparate time zones. The professional services firm, Ernst & Young, for example, has developed KnowledgeWeb, an intranet of over a million pieces of information managed by a sophisticated search engine and used by some 70,000 practitioners in over 140 countries worldwide.

In the same sector, KPMG uses Kworld, a global messaging and knowledge sharing system developed in conjunction with Microsoft. In addition to disseminating information on existing clients, the system allows users to tap into information about potential clients and to gather information on market developments around the world.

The phenomenon is not just limited to professional services firms. Telecommunications giant BT has been developing its own Intranet since 1994, which is now accessed more than 14 million times every month by the company's 85,000 users. The version employed by industrial conglomerate GKN includes facilities termed Innovation and Learning, for sharing ideas on business development, and Fast Forward, which assesses business processes to identify and transfer best practice throughout the group.

For the technology to be effective, however, it needs to provide much more than just a platform for information sharing. According to Craig Ramsay, director of operations at e-business consultancy Scient, it is important to ensure content "comes with both a context and a shelf life. The key challenge is understanding what the end user is trying to accomplish with the content and then delivering the right content in the form best suited to accomplishing that task while keeping the knowledge up to date." Without these controls, companies risk making the information deluge from which we all suffer into an overload.

*The Guardian*

1 Knowledge management has changed dramatically in recent years. This ............................... has meant it has become an important management topic.

2 If things are different and unconnected, they are ............................... .

3 If you ............................... information, you distribute it.

4 If you ............................... information, you collect it.

5 An important, successful, development etc. is a ............................... .

6 If you ............................... or ............................... ............................... information, you can find and use it.

7 If you ............................... information, you evaluate it.

8 The company intranet can provide a ............................... , or opportunity for sharing ideas.

9 Information must be looked at in relation to other information – this is its ............................... , and it is only useful for a limited time – this is its ............................... ............................... .

10 It's important to know what users are trying to achieve or ............................... with the information that they obtain.

11 An ............................... of information is when there is too much of it to handle effectively.

Over to you

How is knowledge shared in your organization or one you would like to work for?

# 32 Intellectual property

## A Copyright infringement

Joe Reggiano is a record company executive:

'Internet users exchange music over the Internet by **uploading** and **downloading** files from each other's computers. They call this **file swapping** or **file sharing**, but if the sites have not made agreements with **copyright holders** to do this, it's just theft. These people are **infringing our copyright**. We need to be able to continue to sell our **content** – our music – if we are going to pay **royalties** to the performers – its **creators** – and make a profit and stay in business.

We need to find ways of fighting **pirate sites** where people **swap** music illegally. Technical advances mean that **content providers** like record and film companies face a big challenge through **copyright theft** such as this. Their assets – music, films, etc. – are their **intellectual property**. The companies can only be profitable if these assets are protected.'

## B Technical protection

'The problem is that everything on the Internet is in **digitized** form – the language of computers and the Internet. In the past, copying, for example from records onto tape, meant a loss of quality. But now, people can make perfect copies of music or films and there is no loss of quality. We want to find technical means of **encryption** so that records and films cannot be copied. We are working with equipment manufacturers on a system of **electronic** or **digital watermarks** – technical means to identify the source of all material. But of course, there will always be people who find ways of breaking this encryption – our defences will have to become more and more technically advanced.' (See Unit 29)

Note: Another form of 'digitized' is 'digitalized'.

## C Legal protection

'We want a system of **digital rights management** to make sure that people pay for the music they listen to and the films that they watch. We want total **copyright protection** for all our products, whereby we receive payment for all use of our property. We might consider **licensing** – giving the right to people to distribute our music over the Internet in exchange for payment. We want to fight any idea that a record or film can be "free".'

**32.1** Complete the extracts from two letters with expressions from A opposite.

1

> People don't want the hassle of going to a record shop and buying records. The music
> industry, in Europe at least, has been very slow to set up its own download sites. If it did
> this, the (1) ............................. ............................... would be less attractive. (2) ............................. are
> the only way of making money for musicians. The music industry should start thinking of
> other ways of making money from its (3) ............................. ...............................

2

> Making music available to others without the consent of its (4) ............................. is
> (5) ............................. theft and illegal; second, there is a growing number of ways to access
> music legitimately on the Internet rather than illegally; and third, (6) ............................. -sharing
> services threaten the future of a music sector that employs hundreds of thousands of people.

Which letter was written by an opponent and which by a supporter of free downloading
of music?

**32.2** Match the two parts of these sentences containing expressions from B and C opposite.

1 By reducing the copyright protection for
music software,

2 Technology is catching up with the
problem of identifying recordings, and
we are

3 In the future, movies are likely to be shot
on film

4 We know a lot about digital rights
management

5 When e-shopping, look for traders with
an encryption facility to make credit card
details secure.

6 Picsel's revenue will come from licensing

a this technology to other companies.

b and we will be looking to share what we've
learned with other file-swapping sites.

c However, remember that not all encryption
offers the same security.

d developing 'digital watermarks' giving unique
identification to a piece of software or picture.

e the court's ruling weakens the incentives for
creative innovation.

f and later digitized for distribution.

## Over to you

Do you think it's acceptable to download music from file-sharing sites on the Internet?
Why / Why not?

# 33 Measuring performance

## A Financial reporting

Maria Malone is the chief finance officer of a large international media company, based in the UK, with activities in television and publishing. She's talking to new trainees in the finance department:

'As with all companies, investors and analysts want to know how the company is being run and how their money is being used. Each year we produce an **annual report** with three key sets of figures:

- ■ profit and loss account
- ■ balance sheet
- ■ cashflow statement

These are the three key **financial statements** in **financial reporting**. They give the basic information about our **financial results**.' (They are covered in Units 34–37.)

## B The financial year

'Our **financial year** ends on March 31st, although other companies choose other dates. Soon after this, we publish **preliminary results**, or **prelims**. The **full report and accounts** are published a few months later. As a UK company, we also publish **interim results** or **interims** after the first six months of our financial year.'

Note: US companies publish their results every **quarter**.

## C Shareholders, bondholders and lenders

'We use **shareholders**' money to operate and invest in the business. Some of the profit we make is paid out to them, usually in the form of **dividends** in relation to the number of **shares** that they each hold. Our shares are **traded** on the London **stock market**.

We also borrow money in the form of **bonds**. We pay percentage **interest** on those bonds and then later repay the **principal**, the amount of money originally lent to us. Our bonds are traded on **bond markets**.

And we borrow money from banks in the form of **loans**, on which we also pay interest.

Of course, our shareholders, **bondholders** and **lenders** all take a keen interest in our accounts!

The results we publish can affect share prices: good results cause prices to rise, if the market believes the company is **undervalued**. However, poor results often cause a drop in share price, as investors feel the company is **overvalued**.'

> BrE: shareholder;
> AmE: shareholder / stockholder

**33.1** Complete the crossword with appropriate forms of expressions from A, B and C opposite.

**Across**

3 Reports that are not for the full year. (8)

7 and 6 down What investors are basically interested in. (9,7)

8 One of the three key financial statements. (8,9)

11 Money lent by a bank. (4)

12 People and institutions that own bonds. (11)

13 The money you pay on a loan. (8)

14 See 2 down.

**Down**

1 Another of the three key financial statements. (7,5)

2 and 14 across Another of the three key financial statements. (6,3,4,7)

4 Together, these people and institutions are the owners of the company. (12)

5 Period of three months. (7)

6 See 7 across.

9 The publication of results: financial ................ . (9)

10 Banks and others that loan money. (7)

**33.2** Complete the table with words from B and C opposite and related forms. Put a stress mark in front of the stressed syllable in each word of more than one syllable. (The first one has been done for you.)

| Verb | Noun – thing | Noun – person/organization |
|---|---|---|
| 'borrow | 'borrowing | 'borrower |
| finance | | |
| lend | | |

**33.3** Complete the sentences with appropriate forms of 'finance'. (There are two possibilities for one of the gaps.)

1 A millionaire ............................... donated a large sum to the charity.

2 The ............................... for the project is coming from two different sources: bank loans and a new share issue.

3 The company must keep a careful control on its ............................... this year in order to avoid making a loss.

Over to you

Obtain the annual report of an organization you are interested in. (Many are available on the Internet at www.carol.co.uk. You can also use this source for other units on Company Finance.) Identify the profit and loss account (or the income statement), the balance sheet and the cashflow statement. What other information does the report contain?

# 34 Profit and loss account

## A Accruals accounting

Maria Malone continues:

'The **accruals principle** means that events in a particular **reporting period**, for example sales of goods or purchases of supplies, are recorded in that period, rather than when money is actually received or paid out; this may happen in a later period.'

## B Profit and loss

'The **profit and loss (P&L) account** records the money we make (or lose!) during a particular reporting period, using the accruals principle. In our case, our accounts record **sales** from books, magazines, television advertising, etc. during the period – this is the money received from sales, minus the labour and cost of materials used to produce them, which is called the **cost of goods sold (COGS)**.

Then we take away **selling and general expenses** – the costs related to making these sales – employees' salaries, rent for buildings, etc. There is also the cost of **depreciation** – this is not an actual sum of money paid out, but is shown in the accounts to allow for the way that machinery wears out and declines in value over time and will have to be replaced. (See Unit 35) This leaves us with our **operating profit**.

Then we subtract the **interest payable** on money we have borrowed in the form of bonds and bank loans. This gives the **profit on ordinary activities before tax**, or **pre-tax profit**.

Sometimes there are **exceptional items** to report, for example the cost of closing a particular operation, but fortunately this does not happen very often.

Of course, we pay tax on our profits and in the UK this is called **corporation tax**.

Note: Sales are also referred to as **turnover** in BrE. The profit and loss account is called the **income statement** in the USA.

## C Earnings

'From the **profit after tax**, also referred to as **earnings**, we usually pay **dividends** to shareholders, and you can see the figure for **dividends per share**. However, when business is bad, we may not do this – we may **omit, pass** or **skip the dividend**.

Naturally, we don't pay out all our profit in dividends. We keep some to invest in our future activities – these are **retained earnings**, or **reserves**.

You can look at profitability in terms of **earnings per share (EPS)**, even if some of these earnings are retained and not paid out in dividends.'

**34.1** Match the words in the box to make expressions from A, B and C opposite. (The first one has been done for you.)

accruals    periods    exceptional    earnings    items    account

interest    payable    operating    P&L    profit

reporting    retained    expenses    principle    selling and general

Now complete each sentence with the correct expression.

1 Our financial year runs from 1 April to 31 March and is made up of two six-month

............................ ............................ .

2 The company's ............................ ............................ has increased by 10 per cent this year.

3 We have decided to keep £25,000 from our profits as ............................ ............................ and not distribute this to the shareholders.

4 One of the ............................ ............................ in the profit and loss account this year related to the restructuring costs of our operations in Korea.

**34.2** Read the profit and loss account for a UK company. Then look at A, B and C opposite and say if the statements below are true or false. All figures are pounds sterling.

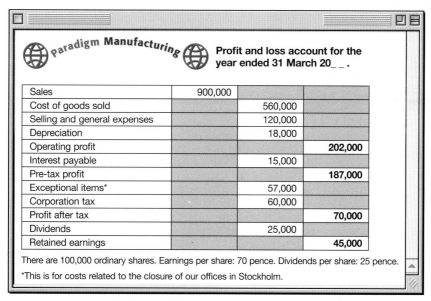

**Paradigm Manufacturing**

**Profit and loss account for the year ended 31 March 20_ _ .**

| | | | |
|---|---|---|---|
| Sales | 900,000 | | |
| Cost of goods sold | | 560,000 | |
| Selling and general expenses | | 120,000 | |
| Depreciation | | 18,000 | |
| Operating profit | | | 202,000 |
| Interest payable | | 15,000 | |
| Pre-tax profit | | | 187,000 |
| Exceptional items* | | 57,000 | |
| Corporation tax | | 60,000 | |
| Profit after tax | | | 70,000 |
| Dividends | | 25,000 | |
| Retained earnings | | | 45,000 |

There are 100,000 ordinary shares. Earnings per share: 70 pence. Dividends per share: 25 pence.

*This is for costs related to the closure of our offices in Stockholm.

1 The £120,000 for selling and general expenses includes the salaries of the salesforce.
2 The £18,000 for depreciation represents an actual amount of money paid out to suppliers.
3 The company has a bank loan and/or is paying interest to holders of its bonds.
4 £57,000 for exceptional items is probably paid out every year.
5 The company has paid out more to shareholders this year than it has kept for future investment and/or future payouts.

*Over to you*

Obtain the annual report of an organization you are interested in. Relate what you find in the profit and loss account or income statement with the items in the table above. Then compare the figures with those for the previous year. What differences can you see?

## A Assets

A company's **balance sheet** gives a 'snapshot picture' of its assets and liabilities at the end of a particular period, usually the 12-month period of its financial year. But the snapshot could be taken on any day of the year.

An **asset** is something that has value or the power to earn money for a business. Assets include:

1 **current assets:**

- **cash** at the bank.
- **securities:** investments in other companies.
- **stocks,** of **raw materials, unfinished goods** and **finished goods,** that are going to be sold.
- **debtors:** money owed to the company by customers.

fixed assets

2 **fixed** or **tangible assets:** equipment, machinery, buildings, land.

3 **intangible assets:** for example, **goodwill,** the value that the company thinks it has as a functioning organization with its existing customers, and in some cases **brands** (see Unit 26), because established brands have the power to earn it money, and would have a value for any potential buyer of the company.

However, there are some things of value that are never shown on a balance sheet, for example the knowledge and skills of the company's employees.

> BrE: stocks, AmE: inventories; BrE debtors, AmE accounts receivable / receivables

## B Depreciation

Of course, some assets such as machinery and equipment lose their value over time because they **wear out** and become **obsolete** and out of date. Amounts relating to this are shown as **depreciation** or **amortization** in the accounts. For example, some computer equipment is **depreciated** or **amortized** over a very short period, perhaps as short as three years, and a **charge** for this is shown in the accounts. The value of the equipment is **written down** or reduced each year over that period and **written off** completely at the end.

Computer equipment is usually depreciated over three years.

The amount that is shown as the value of an asset at a particular time is its **book value.** This may or may not be its **market value,** i.e. the amount that it could be sold for at that time. For example, land or buildings may be worth more than shown in the accounts because they have increased in value. Equipment may be worth less than shown in the accounts because its value has not been depreciated by a realistic amount.

Note: The terms 'depreciate' and 'depreciation' are usually used in the UK; 'amortize' and 'amortization' are more common in the USA.

**35.1** Complete the assets table for a UK company with expressions from A opposite, and the relevant figures, using the following information:

- Paradigm has goodwill, in the form of hundreds of satisfied customers, worth an estimated £15,000. This is its only intangible asset.
- It has investments of £6,000 in other companies.
- It has raw materials, unfinished goods and finished goods together worth £3,500.
- It owns equipment and machinery with a book value of £9,000.
- It owns land with a book value of £31,000.
- It has £11,000 in its accounts at the bank.
- It owns offices and factories with a book value of £94,000.
- Various people and organizations, including customers, owe £7,500.

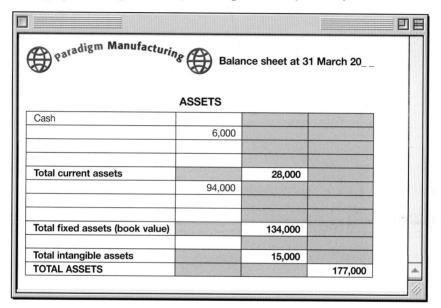

**Paradigm Manufacturing**    Balance sheet at 31 March 20_ _

**ASSETS**

| | | | |
|---|---|---|---|
| Cash | | | |
| | 6,000 | | |
| | | | |
| | | | |
| Total current assets | | 28,000 | |
| | 94,000 | | |
| | | | |
| | | | |
| Total fixed assets (book value) | | 134,000 | |
| | | | |
| Total intangible assets | | 15,000 | |
| TOTAL ASSETS | | | 177,000 |

**35.2** Using the information in B opposite and in the table above, decide if these statements about Paradigm's assets are true or false.

1 The figure for equipment and machinery is the price it was bought for, written down by an amount for depreciation.
2 The figure for equipment and machinery shows that it has been written off completely.
3 The figure for land and buildings is the exact amount they could definitely be sold for.
4 The figure for goodwill is an objective value of the customer base that a buyer of the company would definitely agree to pay.

*Over to you*

Think of an organization you are interested in. What are its main assets? Which of them could be shown on its balance sheet?

# 36 Balance sheet 2

## A  Liabilities

A company's **liabilities** are its debts to suppliers, lenders, bondholders, the tax authorities, etc.

**Current liabilities** are debts that have to be paid within a year, for example:

- **creditors**: money owed to suppliers etc.
- **overdrafts**: when the company spends more money than it has in its bank accounts.
- **interest payments** that have to be paid in the short term.
- **tax payable**.

**Long-term liabilities** are debts that have to be paid further into the future, for example long-term **bank loans** and **bonds**.

> BrE: creditors;
> AmE: accounts payable or payables

## B  Shareholders' funds

When you deduct a company's **liabilities** (everything it owes) from its assets (everything it owns), you are left with **shareholders' funds**[1]. In theory, this is what would be left for shareholders if the business stopped operating, paid all its debts, obtained everything that was owed to it and sold all its buildings and equipment.

Shareholders' funds as shown in a company's accounts includes:

- The **share capital**[2] the shareholders have invested.
- The profits that have not been paid out in dividends[3] to shareholders over the years, but have been kept by the company as **retained earnings**, also called **reserves**.

> BrE: shareholders' funds
> AmE: shareholders'/owners' equity

**36.1** This is the other half of the balance sheet in Unit 35. Complete the assets table with expressions from A and B opposite, and the relevant figures, using the following information:

- Paradigm has a bank loan of £20,000 to be repaid in three years.
- It has issued £100,000 worth of shares.
- It has issued bonds for £30,000 that it will have to repay in seven years.
- It has retained earnings of £10,500.
- It has to pay £3,500 in interest on its bank borrowing and bonds.
- It owes £5,000 in tax.
- It owes £6,000 to suppliers and others.
- On one of its bank accounts, Paradigm has spent £2,000 more than it had in the account.

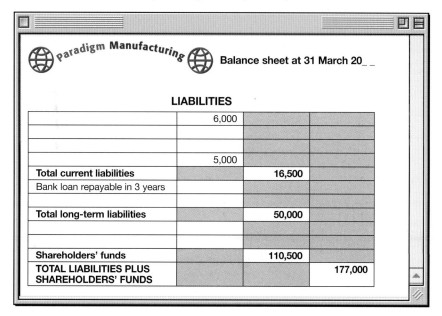

**Paradigm Manufacturing**  Balance sheet at 31 March 20_ _

### LIABILITIES

|  |  |  |  |
|---|---|---|---|
|  | 6,000 |  |  |
|  |  |  |  |
|  |  |  |  |
|  | 5,000 |  |  |
| **Total current liabilities** |  | 16,500 |  |
| Bank loan repayable in 3 years |  |  |  |
|  |  |  |  |
| **Total long-term liabilities** |  | 50,000 |  |
|  |  |  |  |
|  |  |  |  |
| **Shareholders' funds** |  | 110,500 |  |
| **TOTAL LIABILITIES PLUS SHAREHOLDERS' FUNDS** |  |  | 177,000 |

**36.2** Using the information in B opposite and in the table above, decide if these statements about Paradigm's liabilities are true or false.

1 The creditors item includes debts that will have to be paid in two or three years.
2 Overdrafts are a form of long-term loan.
3 In the coming year, Paradigm will have to pay more tax than it pays out in interest on its loans.
4 Paradigm has borrowed more in the form of bonds than in the form of bank loans.
5 Share capital of £100,000 is the current value of Paradigm's shares on the stock market.
6 Retained earnings is the total of all the dividends that have been paid out to shareholders over the years.

## Over to you

Obtain the annual report of an organization you are interested in. Relate where possible the items on the liabilities side of its balance sheet with the items in the table above.

# 37 Cashflow statement

## A Cash inflows and outflows

The **cashflow statement** shows money actually coming into and going out of a company in a particular period: **cash inflows** and **outflows**.

## B Types of cashflow

**Net cashflow from operations** is the money **generated by** the sales of the company's goods or services, minus the money spent on supplies, staff salaries, etc. in the period.

**Net cashflow from investment activities** is the result of:

- purchases of securities (bonds, shares, etc.) in other companies.
- money received from sales of securities in other companies.
- loans made to borrowers.
- loans repaid and loan interest paid by borrowers.
- purchases of land, buildings and equipment.
- sales of land, buildings and equipment.

**Net cashflow from financing activities** is the result of:

- money received through short-term borrowing.
- money repaid in short-term borrowing.
- money received through issuing new shares in the company.
- money received through issuing new bonds in the company.
- dividends paid to shareholders.

Adding and subtracting the figures above, the company calculates its **net cash position** at the end of the year. Investors check the cashflow statement to see how the company is obtaining and using its cash – how much it made from its operations, how much it has raised through new share issues, etc.

Note: 'Cashflow' can also be spelled with a hyphen and as two words.

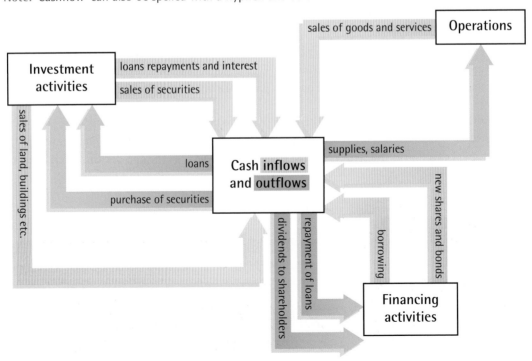

**37.1** Complete the table for a UK company, using the information in A and B opposite, and the facts from the following presentation.

Last year, SBC had a net cashflow from its operations of £550,000. It bought a new office building for £400,000 and new equipment for £90,000. The company lent £35,000 to one of its directors so she could buy a new car. SBC paid £50,000 to buy shares in Company A and obtained £30,000 for shares that it sold in Company B. It received interest of £5,000 on a loan it had made to another director and sold its old office building for £250,000.

SBC obtained a bank loan for £220,000 that it will have to repay next year. It paid out £53,000 in dividends to shareholders. It raised £660,000 by issuing new bonds and £800,000 by issuing new share capital. It also repaid a loan of £180,000 that it obtained last year.

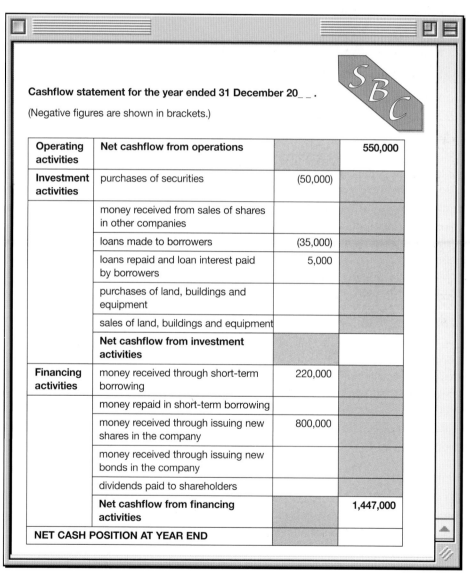

**Cashflow statement for the year ended 31 December 20_ _ .**

(Negative figures are shown in brackets.)

| | | | |
|---|---|---|---|
| **Operating activities** | **Net cashflow from operations** | | 550,000 |
| **Investment activities** | purchases of securities | (50,000) | |
| | money received from sales of shares in other companies | | |
| | loans made to borrowers | (35,000) | |
| | loans repaid and loan interest paid by borrowers | 5,000 | |
| | purchases of land, buildings and equipment | | |
| | sales of land, buildings and equipment | | |
| | **Net cashflow from investment activities** | | |
| **Financing activities** | money received through short-term borrowing | 220,000 | |
| | money repaid in short-term borrowing | | |
| | money received through issuing new shares in the company | 800,000 | |
| | money received through issuing new bonds in the company | | |
| | dividends paid to shareholders | | |
| | **Net cashflow from financing activities** | | 1,447,000 |
| | **NET CASH POSITION AT YEAR END** | | |

**Over to you**

Obtain the annual report of an organization you are interested in. Relate where possible the items in its cashflow statement to the items in the table above.

# 38

# Investment ratios

## Return on assets

Clara Freeman is an analyst at a large investment bank:

'We can check the health of a company by looking at **investment ratios**: the relationship of one key figure to another. The performance of different companies in the same industry can also be compared by looking at the same ratios in each company.

One important ratio is **return on assets (ROA)**, where we look at a company's profits for the year in relation to the value of its assets – its resources – to see how well managers are using those resources. If a company uses relatively few resources in relation to similar companies to generate a higher level of profits, we say that it is **sweating its assets**. But it may reach a point where it is not investing enough in new buildings, equipment, etc. There are limits to how far assets can be made to sweat!'

## Return on equity

'**Return on equity (ROE)** measures how well a company's managers are using **shareholder's equity** (see Unit 36) to invest in activities and resources that generate profit for shareholders. For example, if in a particular year profit before tax is £50,000 and the company has shareholders' equity at that time of £500,000, it has ROE in that year of 10 per cent.

Like all ratios, this can be compared with figures from other companies, or for the same company from year to year. One figure by itself doesn't mean very much.'

## Leverage

'To get a better return on equity, companies may borrow in the form of loans and/or bonds. The amount of a company borrows and the interest it pays on this in relation to its share capital is **leverage**[1]. **Income leverage** is the amound of interest a company pays on its borrowing in relation to its operating profit. This can be expressed as a percentage: for example, a company that makes £80,000 in operating profit in a particular period and pays £20,000 in interest has leverage of 25 per cent. The relationship can also be expressed as a ration in terms of **interest cover** – the number of times it could pay the interest out of its operating profit – in this case, four times.

A company with a lot of borrowing in relation to its share capital or operating profit is **highly leveraged**, or, in British English only, highly geared. A company that has difficulty in making payments on its debt is **overleveraged**.'

Note: 'Leverage' is also called gearing in BrE.

**38.1** Match the two parts of these sentences containing expressions from A and B opposite.

1 The weakest part of the group is the leisure division,

2 Analysts spend many hours studying balance sheets,

3 The company has failed to sweat its manufacturing assets,

4 Brian wanted to learn how US corporations measured performance

a most of which have operated at well below capacity.

b where return on assets last year was only 7.6 per cent.

c and discovered that they all used return on equity as their goal.

d share prices and financial ratios in search of the best-performing firms.

**38.2** Look at B and C opposite. Study the figures in the table for a UK company for Year 1. Then complete the table for years 2 and 3.

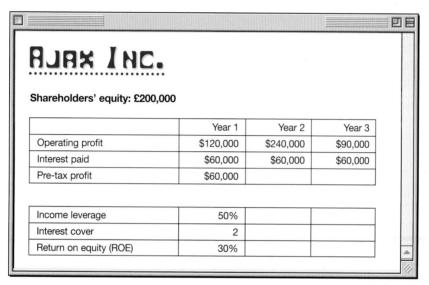

**AJAX INC.**

Shareholders' equity: £200,000

|  | Year 1 | Year 2 | Year 3 |
|---|---|---|---|
| Operating profit | $120,000 | $240,000 | $90,000 |
| Interest paid | $60,000 | $60,000 | $60,000 |
| Pre-tax profit | $60,000 |  |  |

|  |  |  |  |
|---|---|---|---|
| Income leverage | 50% |  |  |
| Interest cover | 2 |  |  |
| Return on equity (ROE) | 30% |  |  |

**38.3** Look at the completed information in the table above. Some analysts are saying that in Year 3 Ajax may be having difficulty paying interest in relation to its operating profit. Which expression in C opposite do they use to talk about this?

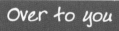

*Over to you*

Obtain the annual report of an organization you are interested in. What income leverage does it have?

# 39 Shareholder value

## Yield

Clara Freeman, from Unit 38, continues:

'Investors look at the **yield** of a company's shares – the **dividend per share** that it pays out in relation to the share price. For example, a company whose shares are worth €20 and that pays a dividend of €1 has a yield of 5 per cent. The dividend per share itself is calculated by dividing distributed earnings by the number of shares outstanding.

Those interested in immediate **income** look for **high-yield shares** – shares that pay out high dividends in relation to their prices. Others might accept lower-yield shares if they think the company's profits will grow over the coming years. These investors are looking for **growth,** increasing profits and **dividend payouts** in the future.

## B Price/earnings ratio

But companies do not pay out all their **earnings** – profits after tax – in dividends each period. Not all earnings are **distributed** to shareholders – companies keep some as **retained earnings.** (See Unit 34)

Investors want to know how well their money is working for them and one way of doing this is to look at the **earnings per share** (EPS). This is calculated by dividing the after-tax profit by the number of **shares outstanding** – the number issued and in existence.

For example, if a company has an after-tax profit of €1 million and has four million shares outstanding, it has EPS of 25 cents.

They can also use the earnings per share to work out the **price/earnings ratio** (**PE ratio**) – this is the share price divided by the earnings per share. The company with EPS of 25 cents and a current share price of €5 has a PE ratio of 20.

This ratio gives an idea of how expensive a share is in relation to the profit the company is making. If investors are willing to pay for shares with a higher-than-average PE ratio, it may be because they expect the company to have higher-than-average profits growth in the future and they are thus willing to pay more for these higher predicted earnings.

## C Maximizing shareholder value

Shareholders in a company obviously want to maximize their **return on investment** (**ROI**). They increasingly look at how the company is managed in terms of **shareholder value** – the total amount the shares they hold are paying out in dividends – and the increase in their value during the time that they hold them.

If a company's shareholders could get the same or better ROI by putting their money on deposit in a bank, they would not be too pleased with the company's managers. So, shareholders watch senior managers' decisions increasingly closely. A company may say that it wants to **maximize shareholder value** and use its assets and potential assets in the most profitable way. This implies key **strategic decisions** such as making the right **acquisitions,** and **divestment** of business units that do not make enough profit, even if they are not actually loss-making.' (See Unit 19)

**39.1** Complete the table for last year for two companies, using the information in A and B opposite.

| | Paragon | Quasar |
|---|---|---|
| Earnings | € 6,000,000 | € 6,000,000 |
| Retained earnings | € 3,500,000 | € 5,000,000 |
| Distributed earnings | € 2,500,000 | € 1,000,000 |
| Number of shares outstanding | 10,000,000 | 5,000,000 |
| Current share price | € 5.00 | € 6.00 |
| Dividend per share | | |
| Yield | | |
| EPS | | |
| PE ratio | | |

**39.2** Using the information in A and B opposite, answer the questions about the two companies in the completed table above.

1 Which company paid more to its shareholders from its profit after tax last year?
2 Which company paid out higher dividends in relation to its share price?
3 Which company had the higher earnings per share?
4 Which company's shares are cheaper to buy in relation to its earnings this year?

**39.3** Complete the sentences with appropriate forms of expressions from C opposite.

1 The committee directed the company's management and financial advisers to explore a sale or merger to determine if either would ............................... ............................... ............................... .

2 The group's bid is the latest part of the strategy formed by its chairman to re-invest the cash raised from its ............................... programme.

3 One analyst expects the company to come to a crucial ............................... ............................... on its shipping business very soon. 'A cool rational manager would stop shipping, as it hasn't made a cent in the past ten years,' he said.

4 Under Karlsson's management, shareholders have seen a 20-fold ............................... ............................... ............................... , and this year the company has been the best performer on the Stockholm Stock Exchange.

5 The engineering group is calling on shareholders for €27.8m to help pay for three ............................... and finance an investment programme.

## Over to you

It often makes sense to maximize shareholder value by divesting loss-making businesses and investing in other areas, but is this always easy to do? Why / Why not? In particular, what issues might the company's senior managers have in relation to:

■ their commitment to the company's basic or original activities?

■ their employees?

■ new activities that they might invest in?

# 40 Accounting standards

## A Audits and their transparency

Every company appoints **auditors**, specialist external accountants who **audit** its accounts. The auditors approve them if they think they give a **true and fair view** of the company's situation. If not, they specify the **qualifications** they have about the accounts. If auditors do this, it certainly gets investors worried!

But auditors complain that there may be an **expectation gap** between what they are required by law to do and what clients and investors sometimes expect them to do – auditors say that they should not be expected to pick up every problem.

Following the scandal of Enron and other **corporate collapses** in the US, investors are increasingly worried about **accounting irregularities**, and they are demanding that auditors should be more strictly **regulated** – the authorities should **supervise** them more closely.

**Regulators** – government agencies checking that the law is applied – are demanding more **transparency**: they say audits should ensure that the company's accounts give a clear picture of its true financial situation.

They are particularly concerned with:

- **auditor rotation**: the principle that companies should be obliged to change their auditors regularly
- **conflict of interests**: some say that a company's auditors should not be allowed to do its consultancy work, for example giving tax advice or doing management consultancy.

## B International standards

In the UK, the way accounts are presented is governed by regulators such as the **Financial Reporting Council (FRC)**.

In the US, they have the **Generally Accepted Accounting Principles (GAAP)**, promoted by the **Financial Accounting Standards Board (FASB)**.

People and institutions invest in companies worldwide. Therefore it's important for financial reporting to be in a form that means the same thing to people all over the world. That's why accountants worldwide are moving towards **International Financial Reporting Standards (IFRS)**.

These standards will eventually be accepted by the **International Organization of Securities Commissions (IOSCO)** representing stock markets all over the world, including the all-important **Securities and Exchange Commission (SEC)** in the US. This will facilitate investment by allowing investors from every continent to understand the accounts of companies, and to trust them, wherever they are based.

**40.1** Look at A and B opposite. Put the paragraphs of this article in the correct order. (The first is a and the last is e, but the other paragraphs are in a different order.)

a
## Accountants seek to stay glamorous
The government will give the accountancy profession a generally clean bill of health today after a year-long investigation. It has concluded that the structure of Britain's auditing firms, the rules governing their conduct and the nature of their relationship with clients are sufficiently robust to eliminate any immediate risk of an Enron-style corporate collapse here.

c
For the past year, Mr Wyman has been engaged in shuttle diplomacy between London, Washington and Brussels. He has persuaded legislators, ministers and officials that the accountancy profession will not shirk its responsibilities to shareholders, and has argued eloquently that any changes to the structure of the profession must be designed to improve the quality of the audit and enhance the integrity of auditor independence.

b
Today's report is the third tranche of new rules to be introduced on both sides of the Atlantic – all aimed at improving corporate governance and strengthening auditor independence to ensure there are no more Enrons. First came the parallel reports from Derek Higgs and Sir Robert Smith in the UK; then the Securities and Exchange Commission's introduction of new regulations to implement more of the Sarbanes-Oxley legislation; and now the government has weighed in with the findings of its own inquiry. That the accountancy profession has emerged relatively unscathed from such a wide-ranging examination of its role and responsibility, conducted against a political backdrop of fear and retribution, is being attributed to the role played by Peter Wyman, the president of the Institute of Chartered Accountants in England and Wales.

d
However, Patricia Hewitt, the Trade and Industry Secretary, will impose some important changes as she unveils the findings of the investigation. She will make it clear that vigilance is critical to guard against lapses in professional standards, and will demand greater transparency from the big accounting firms. She will insist on clear procedures to ensure auditors do not develop cosy relationships with their clients, but the firms will not be forced to ditch lucrative non-audit work for clients – notably providing tax advice – unless conflicts of interest threatening the auditor's independence are identified.

e
The ICAEW has already introduced measures to guard against auditors becoming too cosy with clients. It has a five-year rotation of lead audit partners, and has established the concept of an independent review partner who can oversee the audit but who does not know the client. Even on the vexed question of no-audit services, the profession can report good progress towards ensuring that the lust for lucrative contracts does not affect the audit relationship with the client.

*The Guardian*

**40.2** Complete the sentences with appropriate forms of expressions from the article above.

1 If regulators have no major criticisms to make of a profession, they give it a .............................. ............................. ............................. ............................. . (para a)

2 Rules that are strict enough to prevent abuses are .............................. . (a)

3 Another expression for a large bankruptcy is ............................. ............................. . (a)

4 If professionals do not do what they are meant to do, they ............................. their responsibilities. (c)

5 If something must be watched carefully, ............................. is required. (d)

6 If professional standards are not kept high, there are ............................. . (d)

7 Relationships with clients that are too close are too ............................. . (d)

8 If a professional cannot act properly because work in one area interferes with work in another, there is a ............................. ............................. ............................. . (d)

## Over to you

Should there be obligatory rotation of auditors as recommended by some regulators? Why / Why not?

# Ethics and business

## A Ethical behaviour

**Ethical behaviour** is doing things that are morally right. **Ethics** (countable noun) are moral beliefs about what is right or wrong. **Ethics** (uncountable noun) is the study of this. **Ethically responsible** companies want to do the right thing in areas such as:

- employment and **community**: they want to pay attention to things that affect all people, not just their employees, in the areas where the company has its offices, factories and activities.

- the environment: they want to conduct business in ways **that protect the environment** to ensure that the air, rivers etc. are not **polluted** and plant and animal life are not **endangered**. (See Unit 43)

- winning new business: they want to get business without engaging in **corrupt** behaviour, for example offering **bribes** – money given to someone so that they behave **unethically**.

Companies want to be seen as good **corporate citizens**, with activities that are beneficial not only for their **stakeholders** – their employees, shareholders and so on – but for the community and society as a whole.

## B Accountability and transparency

Ethical corporate behaviour includes **accountability** – the idea that companies are completely responsible for what they do and that people should be able to expect them to explain their actions. **Transparency** is explaining this behaviour in a way that can be understood by outsiders, and not trying to hide anything. Companies may say that they demand high levels of **probity** and **integrity** – complete honesty – from their employees, and that they do not tolerate any form of **misconduct**.

## C Corporate social responsibility

Companies have long had **codes of ethics** and **codes of conduct** saying how their managers and employees should behave. Now they are looking at these issues in more systematic ways. They are designating executives to oversee the whole area of **corporate social responsibility (CSR)**.

**41.1** Read the article relating to the ideas in A, B and C opposite. Then say if the statements below are true or false, identifying the phrase or sentence from the article that confirms your answer. (The first one has been done done for you.)

# How to become good in all areas

Few companies are clear about how to manage what can be an amorphous collection of internal initiatives and external relationships on social, environmental and ethical issues. Probity and responsibility must be embedded in a company's culture, strategy and operations from the top down. But how can this be done? A new guide from Business for Social Responsibility, a US non-profit research and advisory organisation with 1,400 member companies and affiliates, attempts to answer this by taking the reader step by step through the process of designing a corporate social responsibility management system.

Only a handful of companies have a full CSR management system in place, says the organisation, which advises its members on how to make responsible practices integral to their strategy and operations. Its corporate members, mainly in the US and Europe, have combined annual revenues of nearly $2,000bn (£1,300bn) and employ 6m people. They include ABB, British Airways, Coca-Cola, Ikea, Unilever and Wal-Mart. The scandals in the US have underlined how "corporate responsibility taskforces" and codes of conduct are not enough on their own and can sometimes be a smokescreen.

"Creating and building a successful CSR management system is a complex, long-term project for any company," says the report. "It involves a shift in the way a company conducts business and can be likened to implementing other large-scale change initiatives such as total quality management."

The guide runs through basics such as who currently has responsibility for CSR in the company, why a better management structure might improve things and what "hot-button" issues (child labour, drug pricing) face different sectors. It encourages companies to think hard about their stakeholders, what their concerns are, how credible and influential they are and whether they are a potential long-term partner or a liability.

*Financial Times*

1 Most companies have clear, coherent policies on social, environmental and ethical issues.
*false – Few companies are clear ... social, environmental and ethical issues.*

2 If a company behaves with probity, it has high ethical standards.

3 Business for Social Responsibility has a coherent approach to designing a corporate social responsibility management system.

4 It's simple for a company to add a CSR management system to its day-to-day business.

5 Codes of conduct are enough to ensure ethical behaviour.

6 The guide says that a company's stakeholders should all be kept happy so that they are all retained by the company over the long term.

**41.2** Complete the sentences, with expressions from A and B opposite.

1 The company was accused of giving ............................... to local officials in order to allow their products into the country more quickly.

2 The company has supported several projects in the local ..............................., where its factories are situated.

3 Voters demanded that there should be greater ............................... in the election process so that they could understand it fully.

4 Following the scandals of Enron, Worldcom and others, there is greater emphasis in business schools on the teaching of ............................... .

## Over to you

Think of a particular ethical issue that concerns you. Write a letter to an organization asking what its policy is on this issue.

# 42 Social reporting

## A Social performance audits

Businesses are increasingly aware of the importance of social and environmental issues for their reputation. Some are commissioning **social audits** relating to their **social performance**; these evaluate the effect of their behaviour in relation to their employees and to society as whole.

Supporters of social audits say that this **social reporting** is as important as financial reporting. They say that it provides important information for all of a company's **stakeholders**. This is part of the wider picture of **stakeholder theory**, the idea that companies have responsibilities not only to employees, customers and shareholders, but to all members of society affected by their activities.

Critics say that a social audit may just be a **public relations exercise**, with no real benefits.

## B Word combinations with 'social'

| | | |
|---|---|---|
| social | conscience | when companies believe that doing business involves moral and ethical issues |
| | issues | areas of concern, such as unemployment, poverty, etc. |
| | justice | the idea that people should be treated fairly and equitably |
| | responsibility | when companies are concerned about the consequences of their activities on the community as a whole |
| | welfare | payments for people who are unemployed, ill, etc. |
| | well-being | when work conditions are good and people are happy |

## C Labour standards

Giovanni Preston is in charge of social responsibility issues at Rancher Jeans, a Canadian multinational:

'A lot of our manufacturing is done by suppliers in developing countries. Companies in the clothing industry are particularly open to criticisms about **sweatshop labour** – the use of underpaid people with terrible **working conditions**, which amounts to **labour abuse** or **labour exploitation**.

My job is to travel to these countries and to check **labour standards**. I go there to check, for example, that our suppliers are paying their workers fairly and that they have a good **health and safety record**, with low levels of illness and accidents. We also ensure that workers are above the legal minimum age to work – we do not use **child labour**.

We are aware that high-profile companies such as ours are likely to be subject to **scrutiny** – seen and judged by people from outside. We know that if we are seen to be **socially responsible**, the company will benefit.'

> BrE: labour;
> AmE: labor

**42.1** Complete the sentences with correct forms of expressions from A opposite.

1 The management has to be aware of its wider responsibilities to the community, not just employees and shareholders, when presenting new proposals. This is sometimes called ............................ ............................ .

2 There is a risk that companies in industries that are more renowned for polluting and exploiting than caring and sharing could adopt ............................ ............................ and use it to highlight their more ethical activities, purely as a ............................ ............................ ............................ .

3 Auditors should also be required to report to a wider interest group than just the shareholders. These ............................ could include bankers, customers and suppliers, potential shareholders, employees and even government departments.

4 A group of experts looking at how company law operates is already considering whether companies should be forced to publish annual ............................ ............................ .

**42.2** Match the two parts of these sentences containing expressions from A and B opposite.

1 Brazilian society is maturing and adopting a model of economic development that balances economic growth, social

2 At present the country has only a rudimentary social

3 The company is expanding its reporting of social

4 Business success can no longer be defined solely in terms of earnings, growth and the balance sheet as social

a welfare system in place to absorb the shock of millions of people being thrown out of work.

b justice and the sustainable use of natural resources.

c responsibility has become both an individual necessity and an organizational requirement.

d issues, and in a recent business statement pledged to safeguard the economic and social well-being of the communities in which it works.

**42.3** Giovanni Preston from C opposite continues to talk about his work. Complete his statements with expressions from C opposite.

1 I know that one of our competitors exploits poorly-paid people working in very hot and crowded run-down buildings. They use ...

2 They don't pay attention to keeping the factory clean or well-ventilated and clearly don't care about their employees' ...

3 I know for a fact that some of their workers are under 14 years old. They use ...

4 There is a very high number of accidents at their factory. They have a terrible ...

5 All these problems mean that overall the employers have dismal ...

6 This sort of behaviour is the worst type of ... (2 possible expressions)

**Over to you**

Find out about social responsibility issues in an organization that you are interested in.

# 43 Green issues

## Environmental pollution

Companies should of course minimize **environmental pollution** – damage to the land, sea, etc. caused by their activities. They should not **pollute** the air with **toxic emissions** from chimneys or with **effluent** – toxic liquids that they **discharge** into rivers or the sea. They should **dispose of waste** in more acceptable ways.

Nuclear power plants are required to monitor levels of **radioactivity** in the air and water around them, but critics say that even minimum levels of radioactivity are unacceptable. And some **pollutants** are **carcinogenic**, causing cancer.

Governments impose **stringent regulations** to force companies to limit pollution.

## B Recycling

Products should be **recyclable** – the European Union, for example, has regulations about the **proportion** or percentage **content** of products and packaging that must be reused and **recycled. Household** and **industrial waste** should also be recycled. Supporters of **recycling** say that **dumping** waste in **landfills** cannot continue indefinitely and that burning waste in **incinerators** is also **environmentally damaging**.

## C Word combinations with 'environmental'

| | | |
|---|---|---|
| environmental | **credentials** | evidence that you care about the environment |
| | **degradation** | damage to the environment |
| | **devastation** | severe damage to the environment |
| | **lobby** | pressure groups such as Greenpeace and Friends of the Earth who campaign on issues together |
| | **standards** | rules that companies and government authorities should follow in relation to the environment |

## D Sustainability

Some industries are directly dependent on **natural resources**, and managing these resources so that they are not **depleted** is essential. For example, deep-sea fishing has to be done in a way that maintains fish stocks and avoids **overfishing**. Ideally, those engaged in **logging** that causes **deforestation** should have an incentive to maintain future timber stocks through **reafforestation**. These industries should be run in ways that are **sustainable** – in ways that maintain the resources that they rely on. (See also Units 45 and 50)

Another aspect of sustainability is **renewable** or **alternative energy sources** such as wind power.

These are some of the **environmental** or **green issues** that companies are facing. Some companies produce reports on these issues that give a more favourable impression than is justified by the real facts. This is called **greenwash** by critics.

> BrE: reafforestation;
> AmE: reforestation

**43.1** Complete the table with words from A and B opposite and related forms. Put a stress mark in front of the stressed syllable in each word. (The first one has been done for you.)

| Verb | Noun | Adjective |
|---|---|---|
|  | car'cinogen | carcino'genic |
| discharge |  |  |
| dispose (of) |  |  |
|  | environment |  |
|  | incinerator |  |
| pollute |  |  |
|  | recycling | recyclable |
|  | toxicity |  |

**43.2** Match the two parts of these sentences containing expressions from C opposite.

1 He led a political campaign against the company, saying its oil production caused environmental

2 According to the environmental

3 If you really want to show your environmental

4 The project will boost Brazilian efforts to fight environmental

5 In the richest countries with the toughest environmental

a lobby, this type of plastic is such a dangerous substance to manufacture and dispose of that it should be banned.

b credentials, there are several household cleaning products that will cause less damage to the environment, but are likely to cost slightly more.

c devastation in the area.

d standards, the amount of household waste is growing more slowly than the economy as a whole.

e degradation in the Amazon basin.

**43.3** Complete the sentences with expressions from D opposite.

1 Illegal ............................. could accelerate degradation or even cause ............................. , which has affected more than 9.8 million acres of forest in the past 30 years.

2 Fishermen are being encouraged to catch alternative fish species because ............................. has ............................. the stocks to near-collapse.

3 The country's society is maturing and adopting a model of economic development that balances economic growth, social justice and the ............................. use of ............................. ............................. .

4 They accuse multinational companies of '.............................' – polishing up their images on environmental issues with brochures and advertising campaigns.

5 Many congressmen are keen to revive research into renewable ............................. ............................. like solar and wave power.

## Over to you

What does your local government authority do to encourage recycling? Does it do enough?

# 44 Corporate governance

## A Board organization

**Corporate governance** is the way a company is organized and managed at the highest level. This can have a critical influence on the company's performance and behaviour.

A company's **board of directors** includes:

- **executive directors**: the **chief executive** and other senior managers such as the finance director.

- **non-executive directors** or **non-execs**: outsiders with management experience who are invited to sit on the board, bringing their expertise and an outside view. Large investors in the company like pension funds may also have **seats on the board** so that they can influence how the company is run.

In some countries such as Germany, there are two boards. Above the **management board** is a more senior **supervisory board**.

## B Separation of roles

Another key issue in corporate governance is whether the most senior job in a company should be split into two or not. Should the roles of **chairman/chairwoman** and **chief executive** be held by one person, or should there be a separation of these two roles?

Some people say that these two functions should be separated in order to avoid concentrating too much power in one person's hands. Supporters of combining the two roles, however, say that this gives the company stronger leadership.

## C Rewards for success (and failure)

Also important are **executive remuneration** or **compensation**. Top executives are **rewarded** for success in the form of high salaries and **share options** (BrE) or **stock options** (AmE): the chance to buy shares in the company cheaply. These highly-paid executives are often called **fat cats** by their critics. Executives say in their defence that share options are one of the **incentives** that can make them perform better.

But they may also be 'rewarded' for failure, with high **severance payouts** or **payoffs** when they leave the company following poor performance.

Executive pay is becoming an increasingly sensitive issue – for example, executive pay in the UK has risen three times faster than average pay in the last five years. Company boards may appoint a **remuneration committee** to make decisions in this area. And in the UK there are proposals that shareholders should have the right to vote on executive remuneration.

**44.1** Two articles have been mixed up. They contain expressions from A, B and C opposite. Which paragraphs make up each article? (The paragraphs are in the correct order. Article 1 contains four paragraphs; the first is a. Article 2 contains four paragraphs; the first is b.)

**a**

## Article 1: Corporate safeguards go back to the board

A large majority of top executives in Britain have given the thumbs down to proposals designed to strengthen the role of non-executive directors in the boardroom. A survey by the Confederation of British Industry showed that 82% of FTSE-100 chairmen feel that their role would be undermined by proposals contained in the Higgs report released in January.

**b**

## Article 2: Rewards for failure are too high, says Lord Mayor

The City needs to tighten up its standards of corporate governance to restore public and investor confidence, according to the Lord Mayor of London, Gavyn Arthur. It was unacceptable for failure to be almost as well rewarded as success and for executives to take decisions designed to trigger short-term share options rather than act in the long-term interests of the company.

**c**

"We have to have an ethos where the long-term stability of the company is what matters most; where it is bad form and seen to be bad form to be taking actions to generate short-term benefits and share options." Mr Arthur is expected to use a keynote speech at a dinner to be attended by Trade and Industry secretary Patricia Hewitt this month to highlight the need to bolster credibility.

**d**

The report from Derek Higgs, a former investment banker, called for an enhanced role for non-executive directors, as part of a stream of proposals designed to prevent an Enron-type scandal in the UK. Specifically, the Higgs report called for an independent non-executive director to chair the nominations committee, which nominates people to join the board, splitting the functions of chairman and chief executive, and the appointment of a senior independent director to liaise with shareholders.

**e**

Ms Hewitt has already announced a review on the issue of rewards for failure. However, last month Labour blocked an attempt by Tory MP and former Asda boss Archie Norman to change the Companies Act to allow directors to challenge executive payoffs.

**f**

But in the CBI survey, most chairmen believed that the Higgs proposals would undermine their position and lead to divided boards and therefore hamper the way they run their businesses. "What the chairmen are saying is that they need to have unified boards, especially in difficult economic times," said Digby Jones, the CBI director-general.

**g**

Chairmen of the FTSE-100 companies can also argue that corporate governance in the UK already meets high standards, building on past milestones such as the 1992 report by Sir Adrian Cadbury in 1992 and Sir Ronald Hampel in 1998. Be that as it may, Enron and WorldCom changed the corporate landscape. Those mammoth scandals led to major reforms in the US, notably the Sarbanes-Oxley law, which had the creation of an accountancy oversight board as its centrepiece. Once the US started overhauling corporate governance practices, the rest of the world was forced to go some way to meeting these new best practices.

*The Guardian*

**h**

Mr Arthur argues that the current situation cannot be allowed to persist. "I can't bear to see failure being almost as well rewarded as success. It is morally wrong for those who have destroyed their company to walk away with an obscenely large payout. It does a disservice to investors and to public confidence."

*The Guardian*

## Over to you

What is the attitude towards highly-paid executives in your country? Imagine that you are a shareholder in an organization that has recently awarded a large pay increase to its CEO. Write a letter to the organization's head of corporate social responsibility (see Unit 41) asking them to justify this increase.

# 45 Ethical investment

## Controversial products

George Unwin is a fund manager for an **ethical investment fund:**

'People and organizations who put their money into our fund want us to invest it in ethical ways. We want to avoid companies that have a bad record on social and environmental issues. We particularly want to avoid certain sectors – tobacco, arms manufacturers, and nuclear power or uranium producers. So we put our clients' money into funds that do not invest in these activities.

In selecting companies to invest in, we look closely at how they are managed. We are particularly interested in issues of **corporate governance**. We believe that well-managed companies make better investments.' (See Unit 44)

## Socially-responsible investment

There is more and more relevant information about ethically run companies that people can put their money into. In the UK, **FTSE4Good**[1] is an **index** of **ethically managed companies**. In the US, they have the **Dow Jones Sustainability INDEXES**[2] – **DJSI World and DJSI Stoxx**, containing companies which are run in a way that takes account of the long-term interests of society and the environment. This concept, known as **corporate sustainability**, is defined by DJSI in these terms:

**strategy:** integrating long-term economic, environmental and social aspects into their business strategies while maintaining global competitiveness and brand reputation.

**financial:** meeting shareholders' demands for sound financial returns, long-term economic growth, open communication and transparent financial accounting.

**customer and product:** fostering loyalty by investing in customer relationship management, and product and service innovation that focuses on technologies and systems which use financial, natural and social resources in an efficient, effective and economic manner over the long term.

**governance and stakeholder:** setting the highest standards of corporate governance and stakeholder engagement, including corporate codes of conduct and public reporting.

**human:** managing human resources to maintain workforce capabilities and employee satisfaction through best-in-class organizational learning and knowledge management practices, and remuneration and benefit programs.

The **FTSE4Good** and **DJSI indexes** give the overall value of the share prices of the ethical firms, and we can compare the performance of individual firms against them.

This is part of the movement towards **socially responsible investment (SRI)**.

(See Units 43 and 50)

[1] www.ftse4good.com

[2] www.sustainability-index.com

**45.1** Complete the article, which contains words from A and B opposite, with a–e below.

## Analysts look at new factors

'COMPANIES that follow better social and environmental policies are simply better run,' according to Matthew Kiernan. This is a controversial view. Socially responsible investment has come a long way and gained (1) ................................

The research process which Mr Kiernan and his colleagues have developed at Innovest is aimed at identifying what he describes as the 'intangible value' of a company, the factors that are not captured in a traditional balance sheet and which explain the difference between a company's market value and its asset value.

While the concept of 'intangible value' is not an original one, Mr Kiernan believes Innovest's research process brings a new (2) ................................

'The conventional wisdom still in many quarters is that social and environmental issues are either irrelevant or even harmful to the financial performance of companies,' Mr Kiernan says. 'Our argument is that

financial reporting in fact shows (3) ................................

Hence his conclusion that companies following better social and (4) ................................

As further evidence of the link between socially responsible behaviour and enhanced profitability, Mr Kiernan cites South African mining companies, some of which have recently announced their decision to provide retroviral drugs to workers suffering from Aids. 'The cost of Aids is estimated to add $4 to $6 an ounce to the price of producing gold,' he says. 'Giving drugs to your workforce may be a good PR gesture, but it will also reduce your production costs and (5) ................................

Mr Kiernan, however, is certainly prepared to promote his own values. 'We are trying to put sustainability issues in the mainstream,' he says. 'I will die a happy man when the Innovest sustainability rating is turned to as quickly as a price/earnings multiple.'

*Financial Times*

a environmental policies are better run. In defence of this argument, Mr Kiernan refers to independent analysis by QED International demonstrating that a portfolio of shares tilted towards Innovest's preferred stocks would have outperformed the S&P 500 by nearly 29 per cent between December 1996 and December 2001.

b rigour and depth to its analysis. The material is aimed more at analysts and company boards than at shareholders with a conscience, the traditional audience for companies carrying out a 'social audit'.

c only the tip of the iceberg. Mainstream financial analysis captures only a very small part of the competitive dynamic of a company, and it's what's going on below the surface that accounts for success or failure.'

d contribute to the bottom line.' He goes on to cite 3M which, he says, has saved more than $900m (£600m) over the last decade from pollution prevention programmes.

e visibility through the FTSE Good Index launched last year. But many investment managers remain unconvinced that green credentials show up positively in a balance sheet.

## Over to you

Do you agree with the argument in the article that ethically run companies are more profitable than those without corporate social responsiblity policies (see Unit 41)?

# 46 Global forces

A

## Paths to prosperity

Since the fall of communism, a lot has been said about **globalization** – the tendency for the **global economy** to function as one unit, with increasing **interdependence** between different parts of the world.

In terms of economic development, the world is divided into:

- the rich **industrialized countries** or **advanced economies** of the **West**. (The West is taken to include countries such as Japan and Australia.)

- the **developing countries** or **less-developed countries** (**LDCs**). Some are **rural economies** with very little industry. Others are at various stages of **industrialization** – they are **newly industrialized countries** (**NICs**). Some of these are **middle-income** countries. And some, such as the fast-growing economies in SE Asia like Taiwan and Singapore – the **Asian tigers** – are reaching the West's levels of wealth and prosperity.

People who want to emphasize the difference between the industrialized and the less-developed countries of the world often refer to the **North** and the **South**. Before the fall of communism, developing countries were referred to as the **Third World**, but this label is now falling out of use.

B

## GDP and GNI

The prosperity of a country is measured in terms of **GDP** (**Gross Domestic Product**), the value of its **economic output**: all the goods and services produced there in a year. **GDP per capita** is the total output of a particular country divided by the number of people living there.

High national income can mean high **living standards** – high levels of wealth for people – but it depends on **income distribution** – the way that money is divided among the people of the country.

Prosperity can also be measured in terms of **GNI** (**Gross National Income**). This includes money coming into a country from investments abroad, minus money leaving the country to go to investors from abroad. This is the new name for what used to be called **GNP** (**Gross National Product**).

C

## Globalizing trends

The supporters of globalization, the way that the world's economy increasingly functions as one unit, say that it will continue to cause growth and prosperity to spread thanks to:

- **free movement of capital**: money for investment can be easily moved around the world

- **trade liberalization**: obstacles to international trade are gradually being removed.

- **shipping costs** that are ever-declining thanks to the efficiency of **containerization**.

- **telecommunications** and **computing** costs that have fallen dramatically.

## 46.1 Complete the crossword with appropriate forms of expressions from A and B opposite.

**Across**

4 High levels of wealth can mean high ................ ................ . (6,9)

10 The way wealth is spread (or not) through the population. (6,12)

11 See 3 down.

12 Abbreviation for 5 down. (3)

13 Some refer to rich countries as the ................ . (5)

**Down**

1 Nation in the process of industrializing (10,7)

2 Advanced economies are ................ . (14)

3 and 11 across Countries depending on agriculture. (5,9)

4 Some ................-developed countries have a more rural economy. (4)

5 The total value of a country's goods and services is its ................ ................ product. (5,8)

6 The successful economies of SE Asia. (5,6)

7 The value of goods and services produced is economic ................ . (6)

8 Between rich and poor: ................-income countries. (6)

9 Some refer to poorer countries as the ................ . (5)

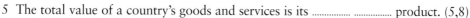

## 46.2 Match the examples of globalization (1–4) to the trends in C opposite.

1 The charge for transporting a whole container of goods across the Pacific can be as little as $50.

2 In today's money, the cost of a three-minute phone call from London to New York in 1930 was £200. The same call costs less than £1 today.

3 There are no taxes on goods traded within the European Union.

4 We can invest in some Asian countries and bring back our profits without penalty.

### Over to you

Can the level of development of a country be measured by GDP alone? If not, what other factors should be taken into account?

Imagine that you are your country's minister for industry. Write an invitation to the chief executives of foreign companies saying why your country is a good place to invest.

# 47 Investment and debt

## A Direct investment

Companies can put money into investment projects in other countries in **private direct investment**. With free **cross-border capital flows**, they can **repatriate** their profits to their own country, or withdraw their investment altogether.

There is debate about whether governments should try to limit **capital inflows** and **outflows** with **capital controls** or whether they should follow the global trend towards **liberalization**.

Some economists say that too much liberalization leads to **instability** in a country's economy, with **foreign exchange crises** which lead to **devaluation** or **depreciation** – its currency becomes worth less in terms of others. For example, some say that China's growth has benefited from the fact that its currency is not freely **convertible**, thus avoiding the capital outflows that other Asian economies have suffered from at various times.

## B Borrowing

The **International Monetary Fund (IMF)** and the **World Bank** play an important role in the development of less-developed countries. A main function of the World Bank is to lend money to countries so that they can obtain the conditions for economic growth. For example, it sponsors **infrastructure projects** – road building, water supply systems, etc. – and projects in health, education and agriculture.

But developing countries may build up **unsustainable** levels of debt and be unable to repay their debts. The IMF has **debt reduction** programmes for **Heavily Indebted Poor Countries (HIPCs)** that will reduce the amount of money that they owe. It also contributes to work on the **Millennium Development Goals** – specific targets relating to **poverty reduction** and the **stimulation of growth** in poorer countries.

## C Word combinations with 'debt'

| debt | | |
|------|------|------|
| | burden | the amount of debt that a country has, seen as a problem |
| | service | making repayments on a debt |
| | justice | the idea that people should be treated fairly and equitably |
| | rescheduling restructuring | when lenders agree that a debt can be repaid in a different way or at a different time |
| | relief forgiveness | when lenders agree that debts do not need to be repaid |

**47.1** Look at the expressions in A and B opposite. Put the sentences a–e in the correct order. (The first is a.)

a
> A ban on capital controls is a bad trade-off.

b
> Meanwhile, import prices soar, spurring inflation.

c
> As money is withdrawn, the country's currency depreciates rapidly, which can lead to more investors pulling out in an effort to avoid losses.

d
> This vicious circle spells calamity for the country's economy: capital flows can be, and have often been, perilous.

e
> Because developing countries have relatively small financial markets and do much of their borrowing in dollars or euros they are vulnerable to rapid financial outflows if creditors suspect difficulties in repayment.
>
> *Financial Times*

**47.2** Now match the expressions (1–10) to their definitions (a–j).

| | | | |
|---|---|---|---|
| 1 | withdraw | a | very dangerous |
| 2 | depreciate | b | take out |
| 3 | pull out | c | disaster |
| 4 | soar | d | leave |
| 5 | spur | e | easily affected by something negative |
| 6 | vulnerable | f | cause |
| 7 | perilous | g | lose value |
| 8 | calamity | h | rising prices |
| 9 | vicious circle | i | rise fast |
| 10 | inflation | j | when a problem occurs that causes another problem to occur, and this process is repeated |

**47.3** Match the two parts of these extracts containing expressions from C opposite.

1 Under HIPC, countries have their debt

2 The arrangement with Moscow benefits the West because it involves no debt

3 Half of Africa's governments pay as much per person in debt

4 There's not much point in debt

5 Mozambique, which receives debt

6 Brady bonds, named after former US Treasury Secretary Nicholas Brady, were created in the 1980s as part of a debt

a relief if the money saved is then spent on arms.

b restructuring plan for developing countries.

c burden cut to levels which the IMF and World Bank consider sustainable.

d forgiveness and requires Russia to pay in a timely way and in full.

e service as they spend on health and education combined.

f rescheduling this month, will not be much better off.

## Over to you

Should the debt of developing countries be completely forgiven? Why / Why not? Write a letter to a national newspaper with your views.

# 48 Trade

## A Dismantling the barriers

Ranjit Rao is trade minister for a developing country:

'We believe that there is increased prosperity for all if we can export our goods and services freely. We are working through the **World Trade Organization (WTO)** to **remove** or **dismantle trade barriers** such as:

- **tariffs:** taxes on imported goods
- **quotas:** limits on the number of goods that can be imported.

We particularly want the countries of the North to **open up their markets** to our agricultural goods. **Free trade areas** or **blocs** such as

- the **EEA: European Economic Area** containing the European Union plus some other countries
- **NAFTA: North American Free Trade Area:** Canada, US and Mexico

have abolished trade barriers between their member countries, but they should be more open to goods from outside.'

## B Protected industries

John Newman is head of a steel company in Nordland, an industrialized country:

We have higher costs than many other steel-producing countries and we can't compete with their prices. Some countries are **dumping** – selling their steel here for less than it costs to produce. So we have asked our government to impose tariffs on imported steel.

Antonio Silva is head of a steel company in Sudonia, an industrializing country:

We feel that Nordland is engaging in **unfair trade practices** – from our point of view it's just **protectionism**. We believe in **free trade** – we should be allowed to compete in an open world market for steel.

## C Fair trade

Claire Longdon is a consumer in the UK:

'I believe in **fair trade.** When I buy products, especially **commodities** like coffee or bananas, I look for the **FAIRTRADE Mark.** The **Fairtrade Foundation** makes sure that **producers** and **growers** are paid a fair price, not just the market price, which can be catastrophically low. For example, prices can fall dramatically when there is **overproduction** around the world causing a **glut** in a particular commodity.'

Guarantees a **better deal** for Third World Producers

FAIRTRADE ®

**48.1** Complete the sentences with appropriate forms of expressions from A and B opposite.

1 US and EU business leaders now need to focus on removing .............................. ................................ between the two blocs rather than aim to create a single .............................. .............................. area.

2 He said raising prices by increasing .............................. on Japanese luxury cars would give Detroit's Big Three automakers an excuse to increase their own luxury car prices.

3 The Asia-Pacific economies have been growing and .............................. .............................. their markets. They offer many new opportunities.

4 The European Union warned that South Korea should open up its car market, accusing the country of ..............................

5 If the Commerce Department rules that Mexico is .............................. tomatoes, consumers can expect higher tomato prices because the US will impose .............................. on them, limiting the numbers that can be imported.

**48.2** Look at C opposite. Put the sections of this article in the correct order. (The first is a.)

a

# Sale of Fairtrade products doubles

Sales of goods that promise a better deal for farmers in developing countries have more than doubled in three years, it was announced at the weekend. Fairtrade coffee accounts for 14% of the market in the UK,

b

and chocolate that carry the Fairtrade certification mark. Last November the Co-op supermarket chain announced it was switching all its own-brand chocolate to Fairtrade.

c

and producers a better deal. Total sales rose from £21.8m in 1999 to £59m in 2002, according to figures released to mark Fairtrade Fortnight, which starts today to encourage shoppers to try the products.

d

and the World Development Movement, to respond to the human consequences of collapsing world commodity prices.

e

Harriet Lamb, executive director of the foundation, said: "Rising sales figures show that the public not only trust the Fairtrade mark but trust their taste too." The foundation was set up at the beginning of the 1990s by agencies including Christian Aid, Oxfam

f

representing 4.5 million growers. More than 100 products are available in the UK in the categories of coffee, tea, cocoa, chocolate, snacks and biscuits, sugar, honey, fruit juice and fresh fruit, and are stocked by independent shops and most major supermarkets.

g

The Fairtrade Foundation certifies and promotes products that meet internationally recognized standards of fair trade. It said that Sainsbury's now sells around 1 million Fairtrade bananas a week, and has own-brand coffee, tea

h

The first Fairtrade-marked product appeared on shelves in 1994. Now foods carrying the mark are sold in 17 countries through 235 traders and 452 companies. They are sourced from 360 producer groups in 36 countries,

i

with sales having increased from 13.7 m in 1998 to 18.5 m in 2001. The growth has been made possible in large part by the increasing willingness of supermarkets to sell Fairtrade products, which are made using ingredients that guarantee farmers

*The Guardian*

## Over to you

Should some industries in your country be protected – if so, which ones? Or should all goods be subject to free trade? Why / Why not?

# 49 International aid

## A    Humanitarian aid

When there are extreme situations, **aid agencies** such as Oxfam or Médecins Sans Frontières play an important role. These situations include war, **natural disasters** such as earthquakes or floods, and **famine** – when people do not have enough to eat, for example following **crop failure**. **Emergency relief** is provided in the form of supplies, medical assistance, and so on. This is part of **humanitarian aid**.

## B    Development aid

Aid agencies and donor countries also give **development aid**, and so contribute to economic development through specific **development projects**. These projects may use **intermediate technology** – equipment and machinery suited to local conditions that local people can operate and maintain.

Some of these projects are designed to improve **infrastructure** – a country's water supplies, roads, etc.

Some provide **seed money** for small businesses – the money they need to start up until they become **viable** and able to develop by themselves.

## C    The aims of aid

Development aid often comes from **donor countries**. Some countries are more **generous** than others, giving a higher proportion of their national **wealth**. The places to which aid is sent and the uses to which it is put are influenced by **pressure groups** and **NGOs – non-governmental organizations** – such as the aid agencies mentioned above.

Governments receiving aid are **recipients**. Some donors require the recipients to use the money to purchase equipment, etc. from them – this is **tied aid**.

Many would say that the purpose of aid is **poverty reduction**. But there is a lot of discussion about how this can be achieved. Some experts say that the best use of aid is to invest in projects that contribute to **economic development**.

**49.1** Complete the sentences with appropriate forms of expressions from A and B opposite.

1 In Ethiopia in the mid-1980s, many people did not have enough to eat. This was one of the most severe ..................... of recent times.

2 In 1999, Pakistan produced much less cotton than it normally does because of unusual climate conditions. This is an example of a damaging ..................... ..................... .

3 Helping people in India after the earthquake there in 1999 is an instance of ..................... ..................... and ..................... ..................... .

4 Sometimes only a little ..................... ..................... is required to get projects going – they can become ..................... quite quickly.

5 The hurricanes and flooding in central America in 2002 were one of the worst ..................... ..................... of the last few years.

6 Small wind turbines to generate electricity on farms is one example of ..................... ..................... .

**49.2** Read the article relating to the ideas in B opposite. Then say if the statements below are true or false, identifying the phrase or sentence from the article that confirms your answer. (The first one has been done for you.)

# The great aid debate

Several factors have brought the question of overseas aid to the fore. Public opinion is one, helped by some very effective lobbying by pressure groups, especially on the issue of debt relief for the poorest countries. Ultimately, though, aid has forced its way to the top of the agenda because political leaders have realised that global security and prosperity depend on an inclusive international economy. Letting poor countries fall further behind is dangerous.

Making aid work is now a central but sensitive issue. In the past, both donors and recipients have tended to hijack the debate for their own purposes.

Recipients tend to bristle at the idea that they waste aid money. That accusation, they say, is a distraction from the basic problem that the donors are not generous enough. There is no doubt that rich countries are often reluctant to deliver on their promises to the developing world, whether it be money for aid, or the elusive open markets they continue to argue will help poor countries most. But there is considerable evidence now – and from a wide range of sources – that suggests that poor countries need to take more responsibility for their own problems and that by doing so they could ensure aid helps deliver what they need. Research by the World Bank has shown that aid can be effective in reducing poverty, but only when given to countries with sound economic management and government institutions. In countries with weak economic management, the evidence suggests foreign aid does little to reduce poverty.

*The Economist*

1 A number of things have made overseas aid a topical issue.
   *True – several factors have brought the question of overseas aid to the fore.*
2 The influence of pressure groups has produced results, especially in relation to debt relief.
3 Donors and recipients have until now taken control of the discussion for their own advantage.
4 Recipients accept the idea that aid money is sometimes wasted.
5 Aid can reduce poverty only when economic management in a country is good.

**Over to you**

Find out about an organization involved in a particular development project and make a presentation or write a report about it.

# 50 Sustainable development

## Climate change

Scientists point to the dangers of **climate change**, in particular **global warming**. This is the rise in temperatures in the atmosphere and the sea caused by **emissions** of **carbon dioxide** and other **greenhouse gases** from the burning of **hydrocarbon** or **fossil fuels** such as oil and coal. Some say that the earth cannot sustain much further **industrialization**.

The **Kyoto protocol** of 1997 was designed to put the **United Nations climate change convention** into effect. This originally aimed to cut emissions to five per cent below 1990 levels by 2010. Some businesses complain that these targets will increase their costs, but see section C below.

## Sustainability

**Sustainability** is the idea that the economy should be organized in ways that can be continued without causing **irreversible damage** to the environment or **depletion** of **natural resources**. Businesses should be run not for **short-term profit**, but in a way that takes account of the **long-term interests** of society and the environment. (See also Units 43 and 45)

Developing countries are trying to attain the **living standards** of the industrialized world. Some warn that, in addition to the dangers of global warming, the world's natural resources are not sufficient for this.

Others argue that **renewable, non-polluting energy sources** such as **wind power** will allow further economic growth without causing damage to the environment. Some argue that **nuclear energy** still has a role to play.

These are some of the issues surrounding **sustainable development** in the global economy.

## The triple bottom line

SustainAbility[1], a consultancy, says that the **triple bottom line** (TBL) makes corporations concentrate not just on the **economic value** they add, but also on the **environmental** and **social value** they add – and destroy. (See Unit 42) The TBL is used to sum up the values, issues and processes that companies must pay attention to in order to minimize any harm resulting from their activities and to create economic, social and environmental value. The three lines represent society, the economy and the environment. Society depends on the economy – and the economy depends on the **global ecosystem**, whose health represents the **ultimate bottom line**.

[1] www.sustainability.com

**50.1** Complete the article, which contains words from A and B opposite, with a–e below.

## Energy's future is trapped in the fossil fuel past

In his State of the Union address, President George W. Bush proposed a $1.5bn (£900m) government research and development programme to replace the internal combustion engine with hydrogen-powered fuel cell cars. (1) ...............................

To be sure, the shift to fuel cells and a hydrogen economy will be as significant and far-reaching in its impact on the global economy and society as the steam engine and coal in the 19th century and the switch to the internal combustion engine and oil in the 20th century. (2) ...............................

Most commercial hydrogen today is extracted from natural gas but it can also be extracted from coal and oil. Even the nuclear industry has weighed in, arguing that nuclear power can be used to extract hydrogen.

The White House's enthusiasm for hydrogen suddenly becomes understandable. (3) ...............................

There is, however, another way to get hydrogen. Renewable sources of energy – wind, photovoltaic, hydrogen, geothermal and biomass – can be harnessed to produce electricity and that electricity, in turn, can be used to electrolyse water, separating the hydrogen from the oxygen for storage and later use in a fuel cell. (4) ............................... Why twice? Because electricity generated from renewable sources of energy cannot be effectively stored. If the sun is not shining, the wind stops blowing, or water stops flowing because of drought, electricity stops being produced and the economy stops. (5) ...............................

*Financial Times*

a  By using some of the electricity generated by renewables to electrolyse water and extract hydrogen, society obtains stored energy to use at a future date.

b  Hydrogen is the lightest, most plentiful element in the universe. When it is used to generate power, heat and light, the only by-products are water and heat. But what Mr Bush did not mention was that hydrogen has to be extracted from either fossil fuels or water.

c  If fossil fuels and even nuclear power can be harnessed to produce hydrogen, the Bush administration can have its cake and eat it too.

d  While some applauded his call to create a clean, non-polluting energy source for the 21st century, many environmentalists were less enthusiastic. That is because there is both more and less to his announcement than meets the eye.

e  While this second approach frees us from fossil fuel dependency and is the solution environmentalists have dreamt of for years, it currently costs more to extract hydrogen with renewable energy. That is because electricity has to be generated twice, first to create the electricity to electrolyse the water and grab and store the hydrogen and then to use the hydrogen to power the fuel cell.

**50.2** Look at the following key words from the article and find words which can go before or after them to form 'word combinations'. Two of them have been done for you as examples.

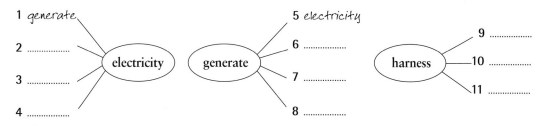

1 generate
2 ...............
3 ...............
4 ...............
electricity

generate
5 electricity
6 ...............
7 ...............
8 ...............

harness
9 ...............
10 ...............
11 ...............

## Over to you

Are you optimistic or pessimistic about the capacity of the planet for future growth? Why / Why not?

# Answer key

**1.1**  1 rewarding, stimulating
      2 client contact
      3 get on
      4 hands-on
      5 No two days are the same
      6 Originality, creativity

**1.2**  1 working on my own
      2 putting ideas into practice
      3 admin, paperwork
      4 team work
      5 snowed under
      6 sense of achievement
      7 bureaucracy, red tape

**1.3**

| verb | Noun | Adjective |
| --- | --- | --- |
| de'mand | de'mand | de'manding |
| 'motivate | moti'vation | 'motivating, 'motivated |
| 'recognize | recog'nition | 'recognizable |
| 'satisfy | satis'faction | 'satisfying, 'satisfied |

**2.1**  1 She encourages us to <u>use our initiative</u>.
      2 <u>Morale</u> here is very good. We feel really <u>motivated</u> to work towards the company's goals.
      3 We have a real sense of <u>responsibility</u>.
      4 We have a real sense of <u>satisfaction</u> in our work.

**2.2**  1 false      3 false      5 false
      2 true      4 true

**2.3**  1 Theory X      4 Theory X
      2 Theory Y      5 Theory Y
      3 Theory Y      6 Theory X

**3.1**  1 salary      4 policy
      2 supervision      5 working conditions
      3 peer relationships      6 security

**3.2**  1 the work itself      4 achievement
      2 recognition      5 advancement
      3 responsibility      6 personal growth

**3.3**

| Verb | Noun | Adjective |
| --- | --- | --- |
| 'delegate | deleg'ation | 'delegated |
| em'power | em'powerment | em'powering, em'powered |
|  | 'hierarchy | hier'archical |

**4.1**

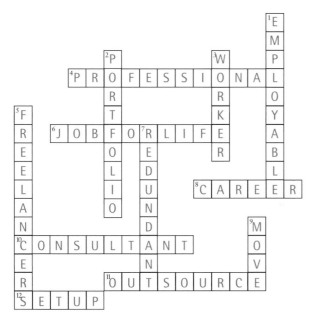

Crossword solution:

1 Down: EMPLOYABLE
2 Down: PROTLIO / PROFOLIO
3 Down: WORKER
4 Across: PROFESSIONAL
5 Down: FREELANCE
6 Across: JOB FOR LIFE
7 Down: REDUNDANT
8 Across: CAREER
9 Down: MOVE
10 Across: CONSULTANT
11 Across: OUTSOURCE
12 Across: SETUP

**4.2**
1 lifelong learning, current trends
2 career move
3 functions
4 consultancy services
5 freelancers/freelances
6 in-house

**5.1**
1 job sharing
2 part-time work
3 temporary work

**5.2**

Nigel: I know what you mean. I don't have the opportunity to <u>hire and fire</u> people as I want! This sort of <u>inflexibility</u> must be bad for the job market. <u>Unemployment</u> in this country is very high.

Melinda: It's a nightmare! If you do want to get rid of people, you have to <u>give them three months' notice</u>.

Nigel: Yes, and you should see the <u>social charges</u> I have to pay for each of my employees just so they can get <u>sick pay</u>, and so on.

Melinda: We should move to Nordland, where they have a <u>flexible job market</u>. The level of <u>job creation</u> there is incredible. Sudonia should copy Nordland.

Nigel: I agree, but it never will, until it's too late!

**5.3**

| | | | |
|---|---|---|---|
| 1 true | 3 false | 5 true | 7 true |
| 2 true | 4 true | 6 false | |

**6.1**   1 stress   2 stress-related   3 stressful   4 stressed   5 stressful

**6.2**   heavy workloads, lack of management support

**6.3**   1d, 2a, 3b, 4c

**7.1**  1 true   3 false   5 false   7 true
        2 true   4 false   6 true

**7.2**  1 critical
        2 expertise
        3 human performance
        4 intellectual property
        5 talent, attracting, retaining
        6 talented individuals

**7.3**  creatives – 1, 3, 5, 6
        suits – 2, 4

**8.1**  1 false   3 false   5 true   7 true
        2 true    4 true    6 false  8 false

**8.2**  1e, 2d, 3c, 4b, 5a, 6b, 7e, 8a, 9c, 10d

**9.1**  1a, 2b, 3b, 4b, 5a, 6a

**9.2**  1 people management
        2 social skills
        3 self-awareness, intrapersonal, interpersonal
        4 self-regulation
        5 empathy
        6 emotional intelligence, EQ

**9.3**  1b, 2e, 3a, 4f, 5c, 6d

**10.1** 1 conformity to specification
        2 quality management
        3 quality system
        4 customer satisfaction
        5 fitness of the design

**10.2**

| Verb | Noun |
| --- | --- |
| con'form | con'formity, con'formist |
| de'light | de'light |
| e'liminate | e'limination |
| ex'pect | ex'pectation, 'expectancy |
| fit | fit, 'fitness |
| 'satisfy | sati'sfaction |
| 'specify | specifi'cation |
| 'tolerate | 'tolerance |
| 'vary | vari'ation, var'iety |

1 (customer) satisfaction       4 elimination of variation
2 (customer) delight            5 (customer) expectations
3 conformity to specification   6 tolerances

## 11.1

| Verb | Noun(s) | Adjective(s) |
|---|---|---|
| ap'ply | applic'ation | ap'plicable |
| 'standardize | 'standard/standardiz'ation | 'standardized |

1 certification, certified
2 application
3 standardized

## 11.2

1f, 2a, 3b, 4g, 5c, 6d, 7e

## 12.1

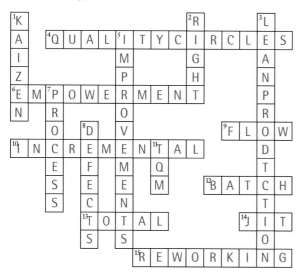

## 12.2

1 employee participation
2 have a voice
3 right first time
4 flow production

## 13.1

1b, 2a, 3d, 4c, 5b, 6d, 7c, 8a

## 13.2

1c, 2e, 3b, 4a, 5, 6, 7d

## 14.1

1 re-engineering
2 fundamental
3 dramatic
4 radical
5 delayering
6 job losses

## 14.2

1f, 2b, 3d, 4c, 5a, 6e

## 15.1

1 performance, benchmark
2 reverse engineering
3 benchmarking, best practices
4 competitive benchmarking
5 Functional benchmarking

## 15.2

1 yes
2 yes
3 no
4 no
5 yes
6 no
7 no
8 no
9 yes

**16.1**

1 strategic move
2 resources, planning
3 resource allocation
4 strategies

**16.2** 1b, 2c, 3e, 4a, 5f

**17.1** low-key – it's the only adjective indicating a low level of competition

**17.2** 1b, 2d, 3a, 4c

**17.3**

1 threat
2 advantage/edge
3 prices
4 position
5 pressure
6 strategy

**18.1**

1 industry competitors
2 entrant
3 substitute
4 buyers
5 suppliers

**18.2**

| Strengths | Weaknesses | Opportunities | Threats |
|---|---|---|---|
| Good locations | Improve staff training | Internet booking increasing | Economic slowdown – travel cut back |
| Big enough to negotiate very good prices | High staff turnover | More exotic places – we are planning to offer these destinations | Online travel companies already established |

**18.3**   1 focus    2 cost leadership    3 differentiation

**19.1**

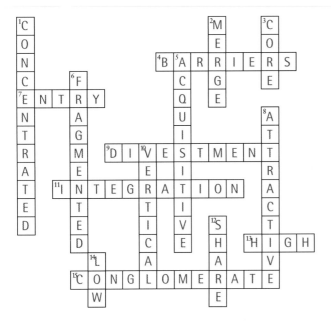

**19.2**

1 strategic acquisitions
2 acquisitions/takeovers
3 subsidiaries
4 unwieldy conglomerate
5 profitability
6 entrants

**20.1** 1b, 2d, 3c, 4a

**20.2**
1 pioneer
2 first mover advantage
3 pioneers
4 follower

**20.3**
1 dropped out
2 shakeout and consolidation
3 dominate
4 mature

**21.1**
1 environment
2 futurologists/futurists
3 the Delphi method, panel (of experts), a consensus
4 forecasts
5 futurology
6 scenario planning

**21.2** 1c, 2a, 3b

**22.1**
1 price
2 product
3 promotion
4 place
5 promotion
6 promotion

**22.2**
1 customer solution
2 convenience
3 communication
4 customer cost
5 customer solution
6 communication

**22.3**
1 false
2 true
3 true
4 false
5 false

**23.1** 1b, 2a, 3d, 4c, 5f, 6e

**23.2** 1c, 2b, 3a, 4d
Sentence 1 sums up the article better.

**24.1**
1 till records
2 anonymous
3 spending
4 log
5 released
6 behaviour

**24.2** 1d, 2a, 3b, 4c

**25.1**
1 segmentation, segments
2 target group
3 ACORN, social class, demographic segmentation
4 behavioural segmentation
5 target groups

**25.2** 2a, 3b, 4f, 5d, 6e

**26.1**
1 brands
2 positioning
3 promise
4 equity
5 branding

**26.2**

1 face-to-face, remote, house calls, personable
2 trust, touch, promise
3 damaged, disappointed

**26.3**

1
a house calls
b telephone/Internet
2 Brand equity is lost and brand promise is broken.
3
a hang up their hats
b mirrors a move
c another nail in the coffin

**26.4**

1 brand positioning
2 brand extension, brand stretching
3 brand dilution

**27.1**

a joint venture, joint venture
b indirect export, agents
c direct investment, direct investment
d licensing agreement, licensing agreement, under licence, joint venture
e export manager, agent, direct export, export manager

Order: b, d, a, c, e

**27.2**  1b, 2a, 3b

**28.1**

```
                 ¹P           ²C                    ³L A ⁴W
           ⁵C    E            O      ⁶H       ⁷H        I
      ⁸T H  I  R  D  G  E  N  E  R  A  T  I  O  N        R
           I    S            F      N       T          E
           P    O            E      D       S          L
                N            R      H       P          E
      ⁹L O  C  A  L  A  R  E  A  N  E  T  W  O  R  K  S  S
           L                N      L       T          S
                            C      D       ¹⁰A
           ¹¹L A  N  D  L  I  N  E  S        C
      ¹²M              N      ¹³D            C
      ¹⁴C O  M  P  U  T  I  N  G  P  O  W  E  R        E
      O                      V      S
      R     ¹⁵D O  W  N  L  O  A  D  F  I  L  E  S
      E        I             C
      S        F      ¹⁷M O  B  I  L  E        S
               I             S
```

**28.2**  c

**29.1**
1 Hackers
2 denial of service attack
3 firewalls / anti-virus programs
4 encryption
5 cybercrime
6 viruses

**29.2**
1 Surveillance
2 human rights law
3 surveillance
4 law enforcement agencies
5 privacy
6 Law enforcement agencies

**29.3**
1 untenable
2 raft of measures
3 stockpile
4 submission
5 climate change
6 strike a better balance
7 exempt from

**30.1**
1c, 2d, 3b, 4e, 5f, 6a

**30.2**
1 clicks-and-mortar
2 bricks-and-mortar outlets, pure e-tailing
3 infrastructure, e-fulfilment
4 private exchange
5 public exchange
6 reverse auction
7 e-marketplace / trading hub / trading platform

**31.1**
1 metamorphosis
2 disparate
3 disseminate
4 gather
5 phenomenon
6 access, tap into
7 assess
8 platform
9 context, shelf life
10 accomplish
11 deluge

**32.1**
1 pirate sites
2 Royalties
3 intellectual property
4 creators
5 copyright
6 file

opponent – 2
supporter – 1

**32.2**
1e, 2d, 3f, 4b, 5c, 6a

## 33.1

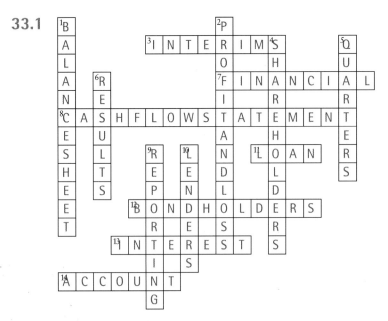

## 33.2

| Verb | Noun – thing | Noun – person/organization |
|---|---|---|
| 'finance | 'finance<br>'finances<br>'financing | fi'nancier |
| lend | loan<br>'lending | 'lender |

## 33.3

1 financier
2 finance/financing
3 finances

## 34.1

exceptional items
interest payable
operating profit
P&L account
reporting period
retained earnings
selling and general expenses

1 reporting periods
2 operating profit
3 retained earnings
4 exceptional items

## 34.2

1 true     3 true     5 false
2 false     4 false

## 35.1

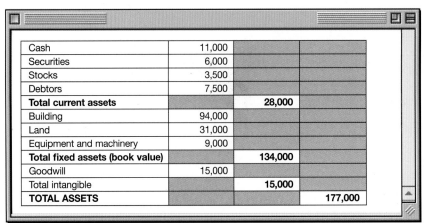

| | | | |
|---|---|---|---|
| Cash | 11,000 | | |
| Securities | 6,000 | | |
| Stocks | 3,500 | | |
| Debtors | 7,500 | | |
| **Total current assets** | | 28,000 | |
| Building | 94,000 | | |
| Land | 31,000 | | |
| Equipment and machinery | 9,000 | | |
| **Total fixed assets (book value)** | | 134,000 | |
| Goodwill | 15,000 | | |
| Total intangible | | 15,000 | |
| **TOTAL ASSETS** | | | 177,000 |

**35.2**

| | |
|---|---|
| **1** true | **3** false |
| **2** false | **4** false |

**36.1**

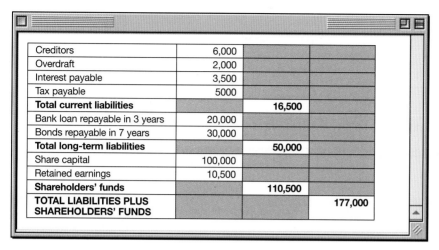

| | | | |
|---|---|---|---|
| Creditors | 6,000 | | |
| Overdraft | 2,000 | | |
| Interest payable | 3,500 | | |
| Tax payable | 5000 | | |
| **Total current liabilities** | | 16,500 | |
| Bank loan repayable in 3 years | 20,000 | | |
| Bonds repayable in 7 years | 30,000 | | |
| **Total long-term liabilities** | | 50,000 | |
| Share capital | 100,000 | | |
| Retained earnings | 10,500 | | |
| **Shareholders' funds** | | 110,500 | |
| **TOTAL LIABILITIES PLUS SHAREHOLDERS' FUNDS** | | | 177,000 |

**36.2**

| | | |
|---|---|---|
| **1** false | **3** true | **5** false |
| **2** false | **4** true | **6** false |

**37.1**

| Operating activities | Net cashflow from operations | | 550,000 |
|---|---|---|---|
| Investment activities | purchases of securities | (50,000) | |
| | money received from sales of shares in other companies | 30,000 | |
| | loans made to borrowers | (35,000) | |
| | loans repaid and loan interest paid by borrowers | 5,000 | |
| | purchases of land, buildings and equipment | (490,000) | |
| | sales of land, buildings and equipment | 250,000 | |
| | **Net cashflow from investment activities** | | (290,000) |
| Financing activities | money received through short-term borrowing | 220,000 | |
| | money repaid in short-term borrowing | (180,000) | |
| | money received through issuing new shares in the company | 800,000 | |
| | money received through issuing new bonds in the company | 660,000 | |
| | dividends paid to shareholders | (53,000) | |
| | **Net cashflow from financing activities** | | 1,447,000 |
| **NET CASH POSITION AT YEAR END** | | | 1,707,000 |

**38.1**   1b, 2d, 3a, 4c

**38.2**

|  | Year 1 | Year 2 | Year 3 |
|---|---|---|---|
| Operating profit | £120,000 | £240,000 | £90,000 |
| Interest paid | £60,000 | £60,000 | £60,000 |
| Pre-tax profit | £60,000 | £180,000 | £30,000 |
|  |  |  |  |
| Leverage | 50% | 25% | 66.6% |
| Interest cover | 2 | 4 | 1.5 |
| Return on equity (ROE) | 30% | 90% | 15% |

**38.3** They say that it is overleveraged.

**39.1**

|  | Paragon | Quasar |
|---|---|---|
| Earnings | €6,000,000 | €6,000,000 |
| Retained earnings | €3,500,000 | €5,000,000 |
| Distributed earnings | €2,500,000 | €1,000,000 |
| Number of shares outstanding | 10,000,000 | 5,000,000 |
| Current share price | €5.00 | €6.00 |
| Dividend per share | 25 cents | 20 cents |
| Yield | 5% | 3.33% |
| EPS | 60 cents | €1.20 |
| PE ratio | 8.33 | 5 |

**39.2**
1 Paragon  3 Quasar
2 Paragon  4 Quasar's

**39.3**
1 maximize shareholder value  4 return on investment
2 divestment  5 acquisitions
3 strategic decision

**40.1** a, d, b, c, e

**40.2**
1 clean bill of health  5 vigilence
2 robust  6 lapses
3 corporate collapse  7 cosy
4 shirk  8 conflict of interest

**41.1**
2 true – probity and responsibility must be embedded
3 true – taking the reader step by step through the process
4 false – creating and building a successful CSR management system is a complex, long-term project
5 false – codes of conduct are not enough on their own
6 false – It encourages companies to think hard about … whether they are a potential long-term partner

**41.2**   1 bribes  3 transparency
2 community  4 ethics

**42.1**   1 stakeholder theory
2 social reporting, public relations exercise
3 stakeholders
4 social audits

**42.2**   1b, 2a, 3d, 4c

**42.3**   1 sweatshop labour
2 working conditions
3 child labour
4 health and safety record
5 labour standards
6 labour abuse / labour exploitation

**43.1**

| Verb | Noun | Adjective |
| --- | --- | --- |
| dis'charge | 'discharge | |
| di'spose (of) | di'sposal | di'sposed |
| | en'vironment | environ'mental |
| incinerate | in'cinerator<br>inciner'ation | |
| po'llute | po'llution<br>po'llutant | po'lluted |
| recycle | re'cycling | re'cyclable<br>re'cycled |
| | to'xicity<br>'toxin | 'toxic |

**43.2**   1c, 2a, 3b, 4e, 5d

**43.3**   1 logging, deforestation
2 overfishing, depleted
3 sustainable, natural resources
4 greenwash
5 energy sources

**44.1**   Article 1 – a, d, f, g
Article 2 – b, c, e, h

**45.1**   1e, 2b, 3c, 4a, 5d

**46.1**

Crossword solution:

Across:
- 4 LIVING STANDARDS
- 10 INCOME DISTRIBUTION
- 11 ECONOMIES
- 12 GDP
- 13 NORTH

Down:
- 1 DEVELOPING COUNTRY
- 2 INSTANTR... (INSTANT)
- 3 RURAL / OUTPUT
- 4 LESS DEVELOPED
- 5 GROSS DOMESTIC
- 6 ASSIST
- 7 OUTPUT
- 8 MIDDLE
- 9 SOUTH

**46.2**
1 shipping costs
2 telecommunications (and computing)
3 trade liberalization
4 free movement of capital

**47.1**    a, e, c, b, d

**47.2**    1b, 2g, 3d, 4i, 5f, 6e, 7a, 8c, 9j, 10h

**47.3**    1c, 2d, 3e, 4a, 5f, 6b

**48.1**
1 trade barriers, free trade          3 opening up          5 dumping, quotas
2 tariffs                             4 protectionism

**48.2**    a, i, c, g, b, e, d, h, f

**49.1**
1 famines
2 crop failure
3 emergency relief, humanitarian aid
4 seed money, viable
5 natural disasters
6 intermediate technology

**49.2**   **2** true – effective lobbying by pressure groups
**3** true – donors and recipients have tended to hijack the debate for their own purposes
**4** false – Recipients tend to bristle at the idea that they waste aid money
**5** true – aid can be effective in reducing poverty, but only when given to countries with sound economic management

**50.1**   1d, 2b, 3c, 4e, 5a

**50.2**
| | | |
|---|---|---|
| **2** produce | **6** power | **9** renewable sources of energy |
| **3** store | **7** heat | **10** fossil fuels |
| **4** create | **8** light | **11** nuclear power |

# Index

*The numbers in the index are **Unit** numbers not page numbers.*

Acronyms are pronounced as individual letters where no pronunciation is shown. (For example: ACORN)

/səˈsteɪnəbl/ 43

'evelopment
ˈ dɪˈveləpmənt/

.ˈ ɔ2

...ating its assets 38

sweatshop labour /ˌswetʃɒp ˈleɪbə/ 42

SWOT analysis /ˈswɒt əˌnæləsɪs/ 18

tactful /ˈtæktfᵊl/ 9

takeovers /ˈteɪkəʊvəz/ 3

talent /ˈtælənt/ 7

talented individuals 7

tangible assets /ˌtændʒəbl ˈæsets/ 35

tap into /ˌtæp ˈɪntuː/ 31

target /ˈtɑːgɪt/ 24

target groups /ˈtɑːgɪt ˌgruːps/ 25

tariffs /ˈtærɪfs/ 48

tax payable /ˌtæks ˈpeɪəbl/ 36

team players /ˈtiːm ˌpleɪəz/ 8

teamworker /ˈtiːm ˌwɜːkə/ 8

team-building /ˈtiːm ˌbɪldɪŋ/ 8

team work /ˈtiːmwɜːk/ 1, 8

technical specifications /ˌteknɪkᵊl ˌspesɪfɪˈkeɪʃᵊnz/ 11

telecommunications /ˌtelɪkəˌmjuːnɪˈkeɪʃᵊnz/ 46

temp agency /ˈtemp ˌeɪdʒᵊntsi/ 5

temporary contract /ˌtempᵊrᵊri ˈkɒntrækt/ 5

temporary workers /ˌtempᵊrᵊri ˈwɜːkəz/ 5

Theory W /ˌθɪəri ˈdʌbljuː/ 2

Theory X /ˌθɪəri ˈeks/ 2

Theory Y /ˌθɪəri ˈwaɪ/ 2

third generation systems (3G) 28

Third World /ˌθɜːd ˈwɜːld/ 46

threats /θrets/ 18

tied aid /ˌtaɪd ˈeɪd/ 49

tolerances /ˈtɒlərəntsɪz/ 10

top management /ˌtɒp ˈmænɪdʒmənt/ 11

total quality management (TQM ) 12

tough competition 17 /ˌtʌf cɒmpaˈtɪʃan

toxic emissions /ˌtɒksɪk ɪˈmɪʃᵊnz/ 43

trade barriers /ˈtreɪd ˌbæriəz/ 48

trade liberalization /ˌtreɪd ˌlɪbᵊrᵊlaɪˈzeɪʃᵊn/ 46

trade unions /ˌtreɪd ˈjuːnjənz/ 5

traded /ˈtreɪdɪd/ 33

trading hubs /ˈtreɪdɪŋ ˌhʌbz/ 30

trading platforms /ˈtreɪdɪŋ ˌplætfɔːmz/ 30

training effectiveness /ˈtreɪnɪŋ ɪˌfektɪvnəs/ 11

transparency /trænˈspærᵊntsi/ 40,41

trendsetters /ˈtrendˌsetəz/ 20

triple bottom line (TBL) 50

true and fair view 40

turnover /ˈtɜːnˌəʊvə/ 34

two sigma quality /ˌtuː ˈsɪgmə ˌkwɒləti/ 15

ultimate bottom line 50

under (a lot of) stress 6

under licence /ˌʌndə ˈlaɪsᵊnts/ 27

undervalued /ˌʌndəˈvæljuːd/ 33

unemployment /ˌʌnɪmˈplɔɪmənt/ 5

unemployment benefits /ˌʌnɪmˈplɔɪmənt ˌbenɪfɪts/ 5

unethically /ˌʌnˈeθɪkəli/ 41

unfair trade practices /ʌnˌfeə ˈtreɪd ˌpræktɪsɪz/ 48

unfinished goods /ˌʌnˌfɪnɪʃt ˈgʊdz/ 35

United Nations climate change convention 50

unsustainable /ˌʌnsəˈsteɪnəbl/ 47

unwieldy /ʌnˈwiːldi/ 19

uploading /ʌpˈləʊdɪŋ/ 32

use one's initiative 2

valued /ˈvæljuːd/ 2

values /ˈvæljuːz/ 25

vertical integration /ˌvɜːtɪkᵊl ˌɪntɪˈgreɪʃᵊn/ 19

viable /ˈvaɪəbl/ 49

video-conferencing /ˌvidiəʊˈkɒnfᵊrᵊntsɪŋ/ 28

virtual organization /ˌvɜːtʃuəl ˌɔːgᵊnaɪˈzeɪʃᵊn/ 7

viruses /ˈvaɪərəsɪz/ 29

vision /ˈvɪʒᵊn/ 16

volume industries /ˈvɒljuːm ˌɪndəstriz/ 18

waste /weɪst/ 43

watermarks /ˈwɔːtəmɑːks/ 5

weaknesses /ˈwiːknəsɪz/ 18

wealth /welθ/ 49

wear out /ˌweəʳ ˈaʊt/ 35

well-being /ˌwelˈbiːɪŋ/ 2

wi-fi /ˌwaɪ faɪ/ 28

wind power /ˈwɪnd ˌpaʊə/ 50

withdraw from a market 16

word-of-mouth /ˌwɜːdəvˈmaʊθ/ 23

workaholics /ˌwɜːkəˈhɒlɪks/ 6

working conditions /ˈwɜːkɪŋ kənˌdɪʃᵊnz/ 3,42

working on my own 1

work-life balance 6

World Bank /ˌwɜːld ˈbæŋk/ 47

World Trade Organization (WTO) /ˌwɜːld ˈtreɪd ˌɔːgᵊnaɪˌzeɪʃᵊn/ 48

written down /ˌrɪtᵊn ˈdaʊn/ 35

written off /ˌrɪtᵊn ˈɒf/ 35

yield /jiːld/ 39

zero defects /ˌzɪərəʊ ˈdiːfekts/ 15

Acknowledgements

Development of this publication has made use of the Cambridge International Corpus (CIC).
The CIC is a computerized database of contemporary spoken and written English, which currently stands at 600 million words. It includes British English, American English and other varieties of English. It also includes the Cambridge Learner Corpus, developed in collaboration with the University of Cambridge ESOL Examinations. Cambridge University Press has built up the CIC to provide evidence about language use that helps to produce better language teaching materials.

The author would like to thank Sally Searby, Joy Godwin, Lyn Strutt, Tony Garside and the team at Cambridge University Press for smoothly guiding the book through the editorial process.

He would also like to thank Caroline Vowles, Paul Buckley and Yuko Hasegawa.

The author and publishers would like to thank the following students and teachers who reviewed this edition: Colin Lamont, Keith Baldry, Helena Sharman, Tim Banks, Julian Wheatley, George Tomaszewski.

The author and publishers are grateful to the following for permission to reproduce copyright material. It has not always been possible to identify the sources of all the material used and in such cases the publishers would welcome information from the copyright owners.

p. 21: *The Guardian* for the text from 'Payouts predicted for stressed teachers' by John Carvel © John Carvel/The Guardian, 5 October 1999; p. 22: Text from 'Devising strategies to prevent the flight of talent' written by Jonas Ridderstrale, published in *Financial Times*, 27 August 2003; p. 26: 'You've got the brains but have you got the touch' written by Helen Pickles, published in *The Observer*, 9 January 2000; p. 28: *Financial Times* for the text from 'Staying in the lead means continually raising the bar' by Morgan Witzel © Financial Times Limited, 23 September 2002; p. 39: The Financial Times for the text from 'Inside track: when quality is not quite enough' by Simon London © Financial Times Limited, 15 July 2002; p. 49: *Financial Times* for the text from 'Intrapreneurship' by Emiko Terazono © Financial Times Limited, 25 June 1999; p. 55: Text from 'Dispensing with loyalty' written by Alan Mitchell, published in the magazine *Brand Strategy*, 29 July 2002; p. 57: Text from 'Second sight' written by Kevin Carey, published in *The Guardian*, 10 August 2000; p. 61 *The Guardian* for the text from 'Death of the salesman' by Julia Day © Julia Day/The Guardian, 12 March 2001; p. 67: *The Guardian* for the text from 'Snooping system is illegal, say police' by Stuart Millar © Stuart Millar/The Guardian, 18 December 2003; p. 73: Jay Berman for letter to editor, published in *Financial Times*, 4 February 2003; p. 89: *The Guardian* for the text from 'Accountants seek to stay glamorous' by Ian Griffiths © Ian Griffiths/The Guardian, 29 January 2003; p. 91: *Financial Times* for the text from 'How to become good in all areas' by Alison Maitland © Financial Times Limited, 11 September 2002; p. 97 *The Guardian* for the text from 'Corporate safeguards go back to the board' by Mark Tran © Mark Tran/The Guardian, 10 March 2003:; p. 97: *The Guardian* for the text from 'Rewards for failure are too high, says lord mayor' © Mark Milner/The Guardian, 10 February 2003; p. 99: *Financial Times* for the text from 'Analysts look at new factors' by Sarah Ross © Financial Times Limited, 11 October 2002; p. 103: Text from 'A ban on capital controls is a bad trade off' written by Jagdish Bhagwati and Daniel Tarullo, published in *Financial Times*, 16 March 2003; p. 105: *The Guardian* for text from 'Sale of fairtrade products doubles' by David Brown © David Brown/The Guardian, 3 March 2003; p. 107: *The Economist* for text from 'The great aid debate' © The Economist Newspaper Limited, London, 23 April 2003; p. 108: Text from SustainAbility website (www.sustainability.com) 'What is the triple bottom line?' written by John Elkington ; p. 109: Text from 'Energy's future is trapped in the fossil fuel past' written by Jeremy Rifkin, published in *Financial Times*, 11 February 2003.

The publishers would like to thank the following for their kind permission to reproduce photographs:

Action Plus p. 42 (DPPI); Alamy Images p. 28 (Mark Dyball/bank queue), p. 45 (George Freeman/SLR camera), p. 50 (Fredrik Skold/crystal ball), p. 52 (Peter Bowater/catalogue shopping); Corbis p. 10 (Jose Luis Pelaez/woman executive), p. 18 (Michael Keller), p. 20 (Helen King), (Tom Wagner/film crew), p. 26 (Left Lane Productions), p. 28 (Peggy & Ronald Barnett/micrometer), p. 31 (Peter M. Fisher), p. 32 (Annebicque Bernard/Corbis Sygma), p. 34 (Lester Lefkowitz), p. 38 (Duomo/pole vaulter, Anthony Bolante/telephone), p. 40 (R. W. Jones), p. 41 (James Leynse), p. 51 (Jeff Vanuga), p. 52 (James Leynse/mobile phone shop), p. 54 (Christie & Cole), p. 56 (Steve Raymer), p. 62 (Richard T. Nowitz/ice-cream factory, Bryan Allen/globe), p. 64 (Jean Miele/satellite dishes, Lito C. Uyan/palm pilot), p. 65 (Roger Rossmeyer), p. 66 (Sausage International/computer data, Philip Harvey/camera), p. 68 (Macduff Everton), p. 72 (Ed Bohon/binary data), p. 78 (Gabe Palmer/fixed assets), p. 84 (Jose Luis Pelaez), p. 88 (Charles O'Rear), p. 90 (Lucidio Studio Inc.), p. 94 (Peter Turnley/river pollution, Wayne Lawler/deforestation), p. 100 (Jose Fuste Raga), p. 106 (Kontos Yannis/Corbis Sygma/flood, Les Pickett/development aid), p. 108 (Paul Hardy/factories, Wolfgang Kaehler/glacier); Corbis Royalty Free p. 74; The Fairtrade Foundation p. 104; Getty Editorial p. 24 (Ruth Gray/Staff); The Image Bank p. 10 (Yellow Dog Productions/teacher), p. 12 (Ghislain & Marie David de Lossy/factory manager); Photographers Choice p. 16 (David Lees); Powerstock p. 12, 14 (age fotostock/car rental manager), p. 45 (age fotostock/digital camera);
Mark Ruffle p. 48; Still Pictures p. 50 (J. Ledesma/UNEP/oil spill); Stone p. 22 (Adrian Weinbrecht/designer), p. 78 (Jay Bryant/computers); Taxi p. 10 (aircraft engineer), p. 72 (Justin Pumfrey/mp3).